OUT OF CONTROL

CONTROL

FOOTBALL'S
WORST
OFFENDERS

Rob Del Mundo

CONTENTS

INTRODUCTION

At all levels of football, from the Friday night lights that illuminate high school fields, to the marching bands that perform in college stadiums on Saturdays, to the spectacle of the professional games projected on millions of televisions on Sundays, the game's star players are thrust into the spotlight of perpetuating idolatry.

But the National Football League – the most popular sports league in the United States – has been plagued by a decades-old epidemic within its fraternity. Too many of its hugely talented players on field engage in criminal behaviour off it. All too often a player's mug shot, and not his media guide photo, is emblazoned on TV screens and computer monitors. The horizontal lines used as height references in a police lineup are seen almost as frequently as the yard stripes on the field. No single demographic is immune. Blacks, whites, Hispanics, rookies who have barely made the team out of training camp, and veterans who are destined for the Hall of Fame, have all found their way into the back of a police car.

In their 1998 book "Pros and Cons, The Criminals Who Play in the NFL" authors Jeff Benedict and Don Yeager published the results of a study of 509 of the league's players and made the startling discovery that 109 – or 21.4% – had been charged with a serious crime.

Fifteen years later, writer Jason Lisk of TheBigLead.com analyzed whether the NFL's Personal Conduct Policy instituted by commissioner Roger Goodell in 2007 was having any positive effect on curbing players' behaviour. The findings were pessimistic. From 2000 to 2006, there were 17.7 arrests per year in football's off-season, February 1 to June 30. Excluding the 2007 off-season, in which Goodell's policy was instituted midway through, the same average from 2008 to 2013 was

28.5 arrests per year, an alarming increase of 61%.

The same analysis attributes part of the increase to the exponential rise of media coverage of the game in recent years. Indeed, the ubiquity of information and exposure from platforms such as Twitter make news more available and accessible and has resulted in greater scrutiny of the players than ever before. Nevertheless, the crime figures are well above the tolerance for a league for which its spokesman, Greg Aiello, said, following Aaron Hernandez's arrest in June 2013, "One arrest is too many."

Criminal incidents have become so commonplace among football players that since 2000 the *San Diego Union-Tribune* maintains its own database at UTSanDiego.com solely for the purpose of tracking arrests and citations that were, "more serious than speeding tickets."

Why does football have such a high prevalence of crime? Three reasons: physical aggression, lack of accountability, and misaligned cultural priorities.

It takes a certain breed of athlete to become a football player. Few people have the determination, willpower, and ambition to run into a 320-pound lineman at full speed. The task is akin to barreling into a brick wall—and that brick wall is hunting you down! Lawyer Douglas Cowan, who has represented several of the Seattle Seahawks' players, opined as much. "Professional football players have to be people who can invoke a tremendous amount of emotion to do what they do. You have got to have a certain amount of reckless abandonment in your personality to do that sort of thing." [1]

Even before a player reaches the pro ranks, he is instilled with the feeling of invincibility. As soon as a youngster is enrolled in Pop Warner football at age five, he learns how to hit and how to take a hit. As adrenaline and endorphins habitually pump through a player's body, the physical "high" translates into a ticking time bomb of hyperactivity in a young, immature mind. Such aggression is inevitably going to be projected in off-field behaviour without any innate mechanism of how to turn off the adrenaline rush once he returns to the family dinner table, or the movie theatre, or the classroom.

As a result, young players are ingrained with a false sense of superiority. Because their social status as football 'stars' gives them a falsely superior sense of entitlement, they mistakenly believe that any transgression within society will be either inconsequential or forgiven.

In one of the more extreme examples, two high school players – Trent Mays and Ma'Lik Richmond – were convicted of rape in a much publicized case in Steubenville, Ohio. Their victim, a 16-year-old girl, had been incapacitated by alcohol while sexually explicit photos of her in her in a drunken state were distributed by Mays, Richmond, and several of their peers on social media. The small town of 20,000 was so focused on the Big Red football team that the players themselves were completely oblivious to what constituted criminal activity. Mays had sent a text message to a friend saying that he wasn't worried about a possible rape charge because his coach Reno Saccoccia, "took care of it." Another of Mays's texts said, referring to his coach: "Like, he was joking about it, so I'm not worried."

By the time high school seniors graduate and enroll in college or university, they are idols in the eyes of fans, meal tickets in the eyes of recruiters, and saviours in the eyes of coaches and athletic directors. They are offered lucrative scholarships, paving the way for stardom in the NCAA and, possibly, the NFL.

These college freshmen are now transitioning into an environment where their opponents are faster, heavier, and stronger than their pimple-faced equivalents in high school. Desperate to retain their roster spots, some young players resort to taking performance-enhancing stimulants. With aspirations of reaching the professional ranks, the pressure is far greater than they could have ever imagined, and their ambitions seem far loftier and more difficult to achieve. Exacerbating the potential for disaster is an environment in which they are not held to an optimal level of standards of conduct.

NCAA football is a billion-dollar industry thanks to the gigantic sums of money that television networks dole out for the rights to broadcast games. In November 2012, ESPN announced a 12-year, $5.64-billion dollar deal to air college football playoffs. The same network has a $1-billion hold on first-tier rights to air NCAA football and basketball games nationally, with the current ten-year contract set to expire in 2016-17.

Given that schools have invested so much money in their football teams, and with so much potential revenue at stake, not only the players, but the coaches, are shielded from any liability, or accountability, for their wrongdoings off field. An examination of the 2000 Rose Bowl-winning team, the University of Washington Huskies, conducted by the *Seattle Times*, exemplifies this dangerous trend.

No fewer than twelve players on the UW roster were either arrested that season or charged with a crime punishable by jail time. Coach Rick Neuheisel, according to the report, rarely disciplined his players, backpedaling on decisions to suspended violators of team rules for fear of weakening his team's on-field performance.

Lawmakers have been just as guilty of catering to the football players' status when almost any other accused in a different vocation would have faced far harsher consequences. One Huskies player was granted bail so that he could return to the gridiron. When another player received jail time, he was allowed to serve his sentence around the football season so he didn't have to miss any games.

Neuheisel, who was fired by the Huskies 2003, resurfaced at UCLA just over a year-and-a-half later. Dan Guerrero, UCLA's athletic director, expressed his concern over the reported violations that occurred under the coach's watch but, not surprisingly, chose to overlook the tainted history. "In the end, it was all about 66 collegiate wins," said Guerrero in reference to Neuheisel's 66-30 record.

This protectionism is widespread. South Bend, Indiana is home to the virtually mythic University of Notre Dame. It was at this institution where Elizabeth Seeburg, a 19-year-old freshman who battled depression, took her own life in September 2010 just days after reporting that she had been sexually assaulted by a Fighting Irish football player.

The player was subsequently cleared of any wrongdoing, and no charges were ever filed in the case. But Notre Dame's handling of the ensuing investigation exemplified an apparent two-tiered system of law enforcement. There was an inordinate delay in addressing Seeburg's initial complaint. Pat Cottrell, a retired officer who worked two decades for both Notre Dame Security Police and the South Bend Police Department, told the *National Catholic Register*: "Just a regular Joe, if they were working a job on campus, I could go there and say, 'Hey, I need to talk to you.'" But when an athlete is involved, he said, "if they don't respond, they don't respond, and that makes it harder to do your job." [2]

Following the Seeburg case, Notre Dame became the subject of an investigation launched by the U.S. Department of Education focusing on the processing of sexual assault complaints at the school. Seven months later, a settlement was reached that allowed the institution to avoid losing federal funding under Title IX, which pertains to civil rights.

The safeguarding in South Bend doesn't stop with the eleven men on the field; it goes all the way up to the men wearing the headsets. Notre Dame coach Brian Kelly was rightfully vilified after a tragic 2010 incident in which 20-year-old Declan Sullivan, a student videographer, perished while filming a Fighting Irish practice from a 50-foot tower that toppled over in high winds. Kelly, who had moved the team's practice indoors the previous day because of tornado warnings, elected to hold the session outdoors on the day Sullivan died. Notre Dame was fined $42,000 by the state of Indiana for putting one of its workers in unsafe conditions and paid for a memorial for Sullivan. However, the university did not discipline any member of its staff, including Kelly.

The hallowed football gridiron is where celebrated coach Knute Rockne inspired his players in a pre-game speech against Army by exhorting, "Win one for the Gipper," referring to the legendary player George Gipp, Notre Dame's first ever All-American. Just before Gipp died tragically at age 25 due to strep throat infection, he uttered those same words on his deathbed to Rockne. With the phrase integrated into sporting lexicon, the prevailing mindset within the institution is to maximize wins on the field. Certainly, the framework of any athletic program is built with the intent of achieving success. But the pursuit of excellence often comes at too high of a sociological price.

Three time zones away in Seattle, the UW Huskies had the same mentality. Todd Turner, who had been the school's athletic director during Rick Neuheisel's tenure, awarded a five-year contract to Tyrone Willingham, Neuheisel's replacement, hoping to restore some integrity to the tarnished program. But Willingham was riled by Huskies fans after winning just 11 of 36 games. Turner, a staunch defender of Willingham, and the Huskies parted ways in 2007. Turner opined that the backlash over the decision to retain a coach with a losing record was a factor in his departure. "Have I been naïve all this period of time? Have I spent all this time working on the student-athlete experience and trying to create better lives for people and our proper place in education, when all I should have been worried about was how many games we won?" [3]

The majority of NCAA Division I college stadiums are located in towns and cities that are geographically far removed from professional sports. Michigan Stadium is in the heart of Ann Arbor, while Notre Dame Stadium is the centerpiece of South Bend. The remoteness from any of the hubs in the four major sports leagues is even more pronounced in places such as Nebraska and Alabama. Much like small Canadian cities where junior hockey is the focal point of the community, the local sports team in the U.S. is the source of attention—and revenue. Restaurants and stores are strewn with flags and banners bearing the logos and colours of their heroes' uniforms. The community is not merely obsessed with the team; it is defined by it.

As a result, any player or team executive is revered.

But, as exemplified by the Huskies' lack of discipline or accountability, when players and coaches aren't held to any conduct standards, turning a blind eye becomes the accepted norm. No account of such egregiousness is more pronounced than the reaction by more than a few students who defended Penn State coach Joe Paterno in the wake of the sexual abuse scandal that rattled the university.

In 1998, Paterno was first alerted to allegations of child molestation by Jerry Sandusky, the Nittany Lions' defensive line coach. Sandusky founded The Second Mile in 1977, a charitable organization that served troubled boys, many of whom came from broken homes. By the 1990s, the foundation had become a vehicle for Sandusky to sexually abuse the very youths whom he had set out to support.

The horrendous crimes took place for more than 15 years before the state of Pennsylvania began investigating the allegations. Athletic Director Tim Curley and Senior Vice President for Finance and Business Gary Schultz, in addition to Paterno, had also been apprised of the examinations into Sandusky's behaviour.

Sandusky was not arrested until November 2011, at which time he was charged with 40 criminal counts. Two days later, Curley and Schultz, having resigned from their respective positions, surrendered to police on charges of failing to report child sexual abuse. Paterno, and university president Graham Spanier were fired the same week.

Paterno's ousting created an uproar from a disturbing number of Penn State supporters of the coach. Some 10,000 protestors took to the streets to light fire-crackers and overturn cars. Riot police were called in to quell the outrage. In the minds of the demonstrators, it didn't matter that unspeakable crimes against young boys occurred while Paterno – whose job description included overseeing the well-being of his team – looked the other way. In their minds, the man they affectionately called "JoePa" won 409 games for the Nittany Lions, including 24 Bowl games in 37 appearances. And that's all that mattered.

Paterno died of complications related to lung cancer treatment in January 2012. Former U.S. President George H.W. Bush marked the coach's passing by saying, "He was an outstanding American who was respected not only on the field of play but in life generally – and he was, without a doubt, a true icon in the world of sports." If a world leader can perpetuate such blind idolatry, it's hard to expect the citizens of the country he once governed not to follow suit.

In July 2012, a statue bearing Paterno's likeness was removed from its prominent position outside Beaver Stadium. If it were only as simple to remove the mentality that props football players and coaches above criticism – or worse, above the law – then academic institutions might be producing fewer graduates who pose any kind of threat to society.

When a player does reach the professional ranks and acquires more wealth and material possessions, he is more likely to acquire a weapon such as a handgun as a means of self-preservation. As more players exercise their Second Amendment rights, the result is a culture predicated on the use of firearms, not just in football, but in all walks of life.

In December 2012, Kansas City Chiefs linebacker Jovan Belcher killed his girlfriend Kasandra Perkins – the mother of his child – then drove to the team's practice facility where he thanked coach Romeo Crennel and general manager Scott Pioli for granting him the opportunity to play for the team just before committing suicide with the same pistol. Following the shocking tragedy, writer Jason Whitlock of FoxSports.com expressed disappointment that the Chiefs' next game wasn't postponed while also addressing the issue of rampant gun use.

"We've come to accept our insanity," Whitock wrote. "We'd prefer to avoid seriously reflecting upon the absurdity of the prevailing notion that the Second Amendment somehow enhances our liberty rather than threatens it. Our current gun culture simply ensures that more and more domestic disputes will end in the ultimate tragedy, and that more convenience-store confrontations over loud music coming from a car will leave more teenage boys bloodied and dead. Handguns do not enhance our safety; they exacerbate our flaws, tempt us to escalate arguments, and bait us into embracing confrontation rather than avoiding it." [4]

Whitlock opined that he believed both Belcher and Perkins would still be alive had the player not owned a gun.

The mixture of uncontrolled physical aggression, lack of accountability, and misaligned cultural priorities is a toxic blend, and the result is a high risk potential for criminal activity. While such factors are not necessarily specific to football, they are prevalent in it because of football's lofty place in the psyche of the average American.

A player has a very short time frame in which to earn possibly millions of dollars while reveling in the adoration of fans from across the globe. For former stars such as Rae Carruth, Sam Hurd, and Aaron Hernandez, the fame has turned to infamy as they serve – or face the near certainty of serving – lengthy prison sentences.

Of the many woeful tales of football athletes ruining their lives, few are more incomprehensible than that of Darryl Henley, who starred as a punt returner and cornerback for the Los Angeles Rams for six seasons, ending in 1994. Henley was charged with conspiracy to transport narcotics after he planted twelve kilograms of cocaine in the suitcase of one of his ex-girlfriends, Tracy Ann Donaho, as she tried to leave the airport.

Donaho, a Rams cheerleader, cooperated with federal authorities to become a witness against Henley. Compounding his already dire situation, Henley, locked within the walls of a federal jail, attempted to arrange the murder of both Donaho and the presiding judge in his case, U.S. District Judge Gary Taylor. Unbeknownst to Henley, his conversations were being recorded by inside informants. A charge of attempted murder was added to his count of drug trafficking.

Henley was sentenced to 41 years in federal prison, to be served at the United States Penitentiary in Marion, Illinois.

"The problem is that everybody believes that it can't happen to them, they'll never get caught," Henley said. "And they look at guys like me who get caught and assume that it must be because I had a background that was worse than theirs." [5]

Henley went to UCLA, didn't drink until graduating from high school, didn't smoke marijuana, and had never been previously arrested. The convict, who now spends 23 hours a day in a prison cell, identified a cycle within a flawed system that cultivates superstars at the expense of refusing to hold offending players responsible for their actions.

"You catch a touchdown against a big rival. All of a sudden you're a hero. Now you're talking to your girlfriend, maybe one of your girlfriends, and she says, 'Why were you with that girl?' 'Shut up!' Pop. You slap her. You smack her. Now I'm out of control." [6]

Citations:
1. "Pros and Cons, The Criminals Who Play in the NFL," Jeff Benedict and Don Yeager, Warner Books Inc., ISBN 0-446=52403-4. Page 235

2. *National Catholic Reporter*, Melinda Henneberger, March 26, 2012

3. *Seattle Times*, Ken Armstrong and Rick Perry, January 27, 2008

4. FoxSports.com, Jason Whitlock, December 3, 2012

5. "Pros and Cons, The Criminals Who Play in the NFL," Jeff Benedict and Don Yeager, Warner Books Inc., ISBN 0-446=52403-4. Page 249

6. "Pros and Cons, The Criminals Who Play in the NFL," Jeff Benedict and Don Yeager, Warner Books Inc., ISBN 0-446=52403-4. Page 252

LANCE RENTZEL

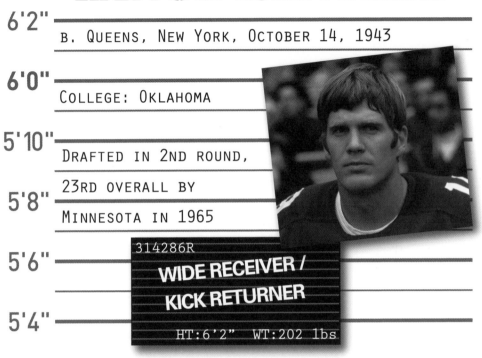

6'2" — B. QUEENS, NEW YORK, OCTOBER 14, 1943

6'0" — COLLEGE: OKLAHOMA

5'10" — DRAFTED IN 2ND ROUND,
23RD OVERALL BY

5'8" — MINNESOTA IN 1965

5'6" — 314286R
WIDE RECEIVER /
KICK RETURNER

5'4" — HT:6'2" WT:202 lbs

IN THE BEGINNING...

Lance Rentzel appeared to be living the American dream. He was a professional football player who was married to a Hollywood star, Joey Heatherton, but his glamorous life masked some dark secrets that – once revealed – sent his life into a tailspin.

Rentzel played college football for three seasons for the Oklahoma Sooners, which were coached by the legendary Bud Wilkinson. Under Wilkinson's regime, the players were often subject to agonizing practices, including having to wear full equipment in extreme heat. In 1962, Rentzel spent most of his time on the bench while Oklahoma advanced to the Orange Bowl. The Sooners were shut out 17-0 by the Alabama Crimson Tide in that climactic game, a Crimson Tide team that was led by future Hall of Fame quarterback Joe Namath.

Two teams in different leagues selected Rentzel in their respective drafts in 1965. Minnesota made him a second-round choice in the NFL Draft, while

Buffalo of the AFL used a sixth-round pick to take Rentzel.

Rentzel chose to suit up for the Minnesota Vikings, where he was used as a kick returner. He had a 101-yard kickoff return in 1965, which set a team record that stood for 42 years. But he was also frequently injured, to the point where his teammates nicknamed him "S.S. Rentzel."

The player also clashed with Vikings coach Norm Van Brocklin. In September 1966, Rentzel was arrested for disorderly conduct after exposing himself to two young girls in a playground in St. Paul. The charge was dropped after he agreed to undergo psychiatric treatment.

Did You Know…?

While Rentzel's most prominent arrest was a shocking story, it caught the attention of one young mother who made the football player the namesake for her child.

Linda Mooneyham, a pregnant, 17-year-old high school student married the baby's father Eddie Gunderson. Gunderson was a reluctant dad who lobbied unsuccessfully for Mooneyham to have an abortion. On September 18, 1971, in Plano, Texas, they gave birth to a son, naming him Lance as a tribute to the Cowboys football player whom they idolized, infamy and all.

When Lance was two years old, his parents divorced. Mooneyham assumed parental control and three years later married Terry Armstrong. Her new husband adopted the young Lance, who took his stepfather's last name.

Lance Armstrong grew up to become one of the most celebrated cyclists, and most notorious drug cheats, in the history of sport. He won seven consecutive Tour de France titles between 1999 and 2005. Having survived testicular cancer, Armstrong became a worldwide hero to legions of fans who supported his Livestrong initiative that raised money to aid patients of the disease.

But Armstrong spent much of his time under the microscope for allegations of drug use. In 2012, the United States Anti-Doping Agency charged Armstrong with using performance-enhancing drugs and stripped him of his Tour de France titles. The USADA also handed down a lifetime ban from competition to the disgraced cyclist.

As it turned out, Armstrong gained far more notoriety than his namesake, Rentzel, ever did.

After the 1966 season, Rentzel was traded to the Dallas Cowboys, with the opportunity to get a fresh start.

 **THE CRIME...**

The change of scenery was advantageous for Rentzel. The Cowboys employed him as a receiver, and Rentzel made a productive transition. In each of three seasons between 1967 and 1969, he finished among the top five in the NFL in receiving yards. In 1969, he was named a Second Team All-Pro and led the league with 12 receiving touchdowns to go along with an astonishing 22.3 yards per catch. On April 12 of that year, Rentzel and Heatherton were married, furthering their celebrity status as an athlete-entertainer power couple.

Dallas finished the year with a record of 11-2-1, which earned the Cowboys first place in the NFL's Capital Division, but they were embarrassed, 38-14, by Cleveland in the divisional playoffs. The following year, 1970, the Cowboys were an underachieving team. A 38-0 pounding at the hands of the St. Louis Cardinals dropped the team to 5-4 in mid-November. Two days later, Rentzel attended a screening of the movie "2001: A Space Odyssey" and became extremely depressed. He searched for an outlet to relieve whatever demons plagued him.

On November 23, Rentzel was arrested and charged with indecent exposure after exposing himself to a 10-year-old girl. Police records alleged that Rentzel drove around several neighbourhoods, spotted a girl in front of her house, then called her to his car to ask for directions. When she approached, Rentzel exposed himself.

The girl's parents were understandably furious and intended to pursue charges against Rentzel to the full extent of the law. The victim's father was a lawyer. Rentzel's family pleaded with the girl's family to reconsider, but to no avail.

WHAT FOLLOWED...

In April 1971, Rentzel pleaded guilty to indecent exposure. He escaped jail time by agreeing to continued psychiatric evaluation, receiving five years' probation. Somewhat inevitably, his marriage to Heatherton ended that same year.

By the opening week of the 1971 football season, Rentzel had been traded to the Los Angeles Rams. The once-proud athlete married to a gorgeous entertainer was now a divorced has-been whose production on the field was in decline. Rentzel never came close to putting up the numbers that he did in Dallas, ending his career after the 1974 season.

During his time with the Rams, Rentzel found the time to write "When All the Laughter Died In Sorrow." The book was written with the recommendation of Rentzel's psychiatrist, Dr. Louis J. West, who thought it would be therapeutic for his patient to chronicle his understanding of his ailment – namely his exhibitionism – that ended up ruining both his career and his marriage.

In the book, Rentzel described being raised by an overly-loving mother, to the point where he needed to assert his masculinity, particularly whenever he didn't meet expectations that he set for himself, such as in a football game. His only method of such an assertion was to expose himself.

ROBERT ROZIER

6'2"

b. Anchorage, Alaska, July 28, 1955

6'0"

College: University of California, Berkeley

5'10"

Drafted in 29th round, 228th overall by St. Louis Cardinals in 1979

5'8"

5'6"

718236R

DEFENSIVE END

5'4"

HT:6'3" WT:240 lbs

IN THE BEGINNING...

Robert Rozier attended Cordova High School in Sacramento. He then went to Aberdeen Junior College prior to transferring to the University of California at Berkeley. Rozier starred as a defensive end for the Golden Bears and was selected in the ninth round of the 1979 NFL draft by St. Louis.

Rozier made only six appearances for the Cardinals, none as a starter, before being released by the team. Drug issues were allegedly behind management's decision to sever ties with the talented defensive end. Rozier played a dozen games in 1980 in the Canadian Football League, suiting up for two games with the Saskatchewan Roughriders and ten outings with the Hamilton Tiger-Cats. He later signed a brief contract with the Oakland Raiders that never materialized into any further time on an NFL gridiron.

The former football player confessed to killing seven people, one of whom was a white male passed out in the parking lot of a bar.

 THE CRIME...

Without any direction in his life, Rozier drifted about the United States. By 1982, he joined a Miami-based cult founded by Yahweh ben Yahweh (born Hulon Mitchell, Jr.) Yahweh presided over an empire called the "Temple of Love" which had hundreds of followers in cities all over the U.S. Yahweh was feted as a black role model and even joined the Chamber of Commerce. But, he lashed out at whites, believing that blacks were the "true Jews" living among "white devils."

Rozier moved into the "Temple of Love" and changed his name to Neriah Israel, or "child of God." In 1985, Rozier joined Yahweh's secret group called "The Brotherhood." Applicants had to satisfy a horrifying prerequisite to confirm their membership. They were required to murder a 'white devil' and bring a victim's body part back to Yahweh as proof of the deed. Yahweh perceived his bizarre demand as simply retribution for historical injustices against blacks.

Rozier's foray into "The Brotherhood" came in April 1986 when he ventured into the Coconut Grove area of Miami with a 12-inch Japanese-style knife. He stabbed an intoxicated man and his roommate to death in order to please Yahweh. Rozier initially considered beheading his two victims to gather the requisite evidence, but he had no means of discreetly transporting the severed parts back to Yahweh. Instead, he presented the bloody weapon to confirm the horrific crime.

Over the next several months, police were baffled by the findings of more white

Did You Know...?

Robert Rozier was an equally bad person on both sides of the border. With the Cardinals in 1979 he played six games for legendary Oklahoma college coach Bud Wilkinson. Then he jumped across the border in 1980 and played two games for Saskatchewan before moving on to Hamilton where he played ten games and had one interception on a team that advanced to the Grey Cup against Edmonton.

The Royal Canadian Mounted Police wanted him for 32 counts of fraud for bouncing cheques totalling between $20,000 and $30,000. "All the while he was playing here, he was passing phony cheques," revealed Sergeant Gary Proctor of the RCMP. "He was running a scam," said Harley Deeks, president of Molson Brewery in Alberta, who went deer hunting with Rozier once. "He used my name to get a bank loan. He was running up huge bills and charging the whole mess to the football team."

men on Miami streets, dead and mutilated. In one instance, a pair of transients had their ears sliced off as part of "The Brotherhood" sadistic ritual.

On October 31, 1986 Rozier was arrested and charged with murder. He struck a plea bargain to testify against Yahweh's cult, becoming a key witness for the United States government. The former football player confessed to killing seven people, one of whom was a white male passed out in the parking lot of a bar. After Rozier and a fellow cult member stabbed the victim to death and sliced off his ear, they lost the ear in the dark going home, so they returned to the scene of the murder and cut off the man's other ear to return to Yahweh.

During the testimony, Rozier said that six of the killings were done on Yahweh's orders, while the seventh victim was a panhandler who repeatedly asked for money and cigarettes. After Rozier murdered the vagrant, he threw the body into a river.

Rozier was originally sentenced to 22 years in prison but was set free in 1996 after serving a decade behind bars.

WHAT FOLLOWED...

Rozier's troubles with the law were far from over. With a target on his back after betraying Yahweh, he was placed into a witness protection program and given the identity Robert Ramses. While living comfortably in the Sacramento area, he was arrested on February 5, 1999, for writing a bad cheque for $66 to pay for an automobile repair.

After police discovered his true identity, they also found a trail of 29 bounced cheques adding up to more than $2,000. His charge was upgraded from a misdemeanour to a felony.

Rozier was also indicted by New Jersey authorities in the murder of 52-year-old Attilio Cicala, whose killing was allegedly performed as a sacrifice for Yahweh's cult. California prosecutors forged on with their case instead of turning Rozier over to the Garden State.

An incredulous Rozier told the *Sacramento Bee*: "I took them [El Dorado detectives] into confidence and let them know who I was. I was a guy who had cooperated with several police agencies and the United States government. I figured they'd think, 'Let's not blow his cover with a cheque charge.'"

Rozier was not only convicted; he was sentenced to 25 years to life in prison under California's "three strikes" law. The verdict was handed down by Judge Eddie T. Keller.

O.J. SIMPSON

6'2" B. SAN FRANCISCO, CALIFORNIA, JULY 9, 1947

6'0"

COLLEGE: UNIVERSITY OF

SOUTHERN CALIFORNIA
5'10"
DRAFTED IN 1ST ROUND,

1ST OVERALL BY BUFFALO
5'8"
IN 1969

373280S

5'6" RUNNING BACK

5'4"

HT:6'2" WT:212 lbs

IN THE BEGINNING...

O.J. Simpson was a standout rusher with the USC Trojans, becoming an All-American in both 1967 and 1968. In the latter year he claimed the Heisman Trophy, winning the award in the largest landslide vote in history. His dominance on the field made him an easy first-overall selection by the Buffalo Bills in the 1969 draft.

The transition from college to the pros wasn't instantaneous or smooth for Simpson. He spent more than a fair share of his first three years in Buffalo on the sidelines. His career finally took flight when the Bills rehired Lou Saban as coach in an attempt to reverse their dismal fortunes. The 1971 edition of the team won just one of its 14 games. Simpson took full advantage of the opportunity to blossom under Saban's tutelage, leading the NFL in 1972 with 1,251 rushing yards.

The following season saw one of the greatest single-player productions in league history as Simpson became the first running back to rush for over 2,000 yards. A handful of NFL players have eclipsed the mark since, but Simpson was the only back to accomplish the feat in a 14-game season. His yards-per-game average of 143.1 remains a league record.

For an encore, Simpson ran for 1,817 yards in 1975 and also registered a career-high 426 receiving yards, setting an NFL record 23 touchdowns (since broken by LaDanian Tomlinson, who found the end zone 31 times in 2006).

Over an 11-year career, Simpson rushed for 11,236 yards and had five consecutive All-Pro selections, ending in 1976. When he was inducted into the Pro Football Hall of Fame in 1985, no one could have predicted the headlines he would make less than a decade later.

 THE CRIME...

On the night of June 12, 1994, Nicole Brown – Simpson's second wife – and her friend Ronald Goldman were found dead among pools of blood outside Brown's condominium in Brentwood, an affluent Los Angeles suburb. As police launched their investigation, Simpson immediately became their prime suspect. The man nicknamed "Juice" who had endeared football fans both on the field for his heroics and off the field for his presence in television and movies, incredibly became the subject of a double-murder investigation.

Five days after the killings, Simpson led police through a low-speed chase along the Los Angeles freeways in a white Ford Bronco before being arrested. It was a scene that not even the most creative Hollywood minds could have scripted.

The subsequent trial lasted nine months. Dubbed the 'trial of the century,' it was the most publicized case in United States history, spurring an unprecedented media frenzy. Millions of viewers were captivated by the trial, broadcast nationally, as Judge Lance Ito, prosecutors Marcia Clark and Christopher Darden, and defence attorneys Johnnie Cochran and Robert Shapiro became household names.

On October 3, 1995, Simpson was acquitted of the murders. Ron Goldman's sister Kim wept openly shortly after the court clerk read aloud the verdict of "not guilty." The outcome polarized much of the nation among racial lines. Black people celebrated; white people mourned.

Simpson became a free man, but it was not his last serious encounter with the law.

WHAT FOLLOWED…

On October 23, 1996, Simpson was once again a courtroom defendant in a civil trial. The Brown and Goldman families were the plaintiffs in a wrongful death lawsuit in which they emerged victorious. Just over three months later, Simpson was found criminally liable for the deaths of the people he was acquitted of murdering and was ordered to pay the staggering sum of $33,500,000 in damages.

Did You Know…?

As his playing career was coming to an end, Simpson was able to use his charismatic personality to pursue a successful film career. He went from starring in television commercials for a rental car company to hosting "Saturday Night Live" to landing a job as a football commentator with NBC Sports.

Simpson's credits include the television mini-series "Roots," and the motion pictures "The Towering Inferno," "The Cassandra Crossing," and "Capricorn One." In an ironic twist, in one of his most famous roles, the man who has been convicted – and (many feel wrongly) acquitted – of heinous criminal acts played a detective tasked with serving and protecting the public.

Simpson starred in the successful comedy series "The Naked Gun," playing detective Nordberg in each part of the trilogy. Nordberg, a clumsy, uncoordinated lawman in the mold of Inspector Clouseau, is a colleague of Frank Drebin, portrayed by Leslie Nielsen. Throughout all of his character's misadventures, including a wheelchair mishap at the end of the first movie, Simpson, in retrospect, appears completely miscast as a law enforcement official.

While Simpson had a few minor brushes with the law in the early part of the 21st century, the long arm finally caught up to him in September 2007.

The full amount was never paid out, as Simpson was broke, according to his attorney. But the Goldman family was reimbursed with at least a modest sum of just over $382,000 when some of Simpson's belongings were auctioned. One of the items sold was his 1968 Heisman Trophy.

While Simpson had a few minor brushes with the law in the early part of the 21st century, the long arm finally caught up to him in September 2007. He and three co-defendants were implicated in an armed robbery inside Palace Station Hotel and Casino in Las Vegas. Simpson claimed that he was attempting to retrieve memorabilia that had been stolen from him but denied brandishing a weapon during the confrontation. His denials fell on deaf ears as his other co-defendants arranged for plea bargains for reduced sentences in exchange for testimony against Simpson.

In 2008 – exactly 13 years to the day of his double-murder acquittal – Simpson was convicted of armed robbery, kidnapping, and assault. He was sentenced to 33 years in prison, with the possibility of parole after nine years.

WARREN MOON

6'2"

B. LOS ANGELES, CALIFORNIA, NOVEMBER 18, 1956

6'0"

COLLEGE: WASHINGTON

5'10"

UNDRAFTED. SIGNED BY

HOUSTON OILERS AS A

5'8"

FREE AGENT IN 1984.

994276M

5'6"

QUARTERBACK

5'4"

HT:6'3"   WT:218 lbs

IN THE BEGINNING...

Whether in college, or the CFL, or the NFL, Warren Moon excelled everywhere he played. He led the University of Washington Huskies to a Rose Bowl victory at the end of a glorious 1977 season in which he was named Pac-8 player of the year. But unlike today's NFL, teams were skeptical about drafting a quarterback who was black. At the time Moon was being professionally scouted, James Harris, who turned pro in 1969, had been the only African-American quarterback with any success in the league.

Thus, at the 1978 draft, Moon – the reigning Rose Bowl MVP – was, incredibly, passed over. Ignored altogether. Undeterred, Moon took his craft north of the border to play for the Edmonton Eskimos in the CFL. Under legendary coach Hugh Campbell, Moon was the driving force behind an unprecedented five consecutive Grey Cup championships for Edmonton from 1978 to 1982.

Following a six-year CFL career in which he threw for 21,228 yards and 144 touchdowns, Moon finally joined the NFL in 1984, signing with Houston. He immediately began rewriting the Oilers' record books, setting a club mark with 3,338 passing yards in his first year with the team. Although Houston had losing records in each of Moon's first three seasons, by 1987 the team had adopted a more offensive style of play and started winning consistently. Moon's reputation soared to the point that he was named to his first of nine career Pro Bowl games in 1988.

The year 1990 was a banner one for Moon as he led the league in passing yards (4,689) and passing touchdowns (33). He was named the NFL Walter Payton man of the year and also the *Associated Press* offensive player of the year. For an encore, Moon threw for 4,690 yards in 1991, becoming only the third player in league history – after Dan Fouts and Dan Marino – to eclipse the 4,000-yard passing mark in consecutive years.

After a decade in Houston, Moon was traded to the Minnesota Vikings in 1994. While he continued his elite play, he was also masking some hidden off-field turmoil.

Did You Know...?

Moon was elected into the Pro Football Hall of Fame in 2006 in his first year of eligibility. He is the first black quarterback, first CFL alumnus, and first undrafted quarterback to be enshrined in Canton, Ohio.

At the time of his retirement, Moon led all professional quarterbacks with 70,553 career passing yards, the sum of his NFL and CFL totals, representing a record. Moon held the mark until 2006 when Toronto's Damon Allen surpassed it at the traditional Labour Day game between the Argonauts and Hamilton Tiger-Cats at Ivor Wynne Stadium. Allen's totals were all accumulated in the CFL, and when he retired he had 72,381 passing yards to his credit.

Brett Favre is the NFL's all-time leader in that category at 71,838, sitting in third place. The current title of professional football's all-time leading passer goes to Anthony Calvillo, who accumulated 79,816 over a 20-year CFL career that ended with his retirement in January 2014.

THE CRIME...

On June 18, 1995, police in Missouri City, Texas, were called to the Moon house-hold after the youngest of his four children, seven-year-old Jeffrey, placed a 911 call. An argument between Moon and his wife Felicia had turned violent when – according to Felicia's statement – her husband struck her in the head and choked her to the point of losing consciousness. She had bruises and scratches on her face, neck, leg, and back.

Three days later, Moon was arrested and charged with assault. He was released on a $1,000 bond. The episode dominated the news headlines in Houston where he still enjoyed celebrity status despite no longer playing for the Oilers. Moon had built up a strong network in the city by being involved in several charitable endeavours, creating the Crescent Moon Foundation with Felicia to help provide scholarships to high-school students in need.

Addressing the media, Moon apologized to Felicia and his family prior to his booking at the police station. "One of the goals for myself had always been not to get arrested in my life for anything," Moon told the *New York Times*. "The finger-printing. Taking the mug shots. It is something I will never forget, something you can never prepare for. But I must say that it set into quicker motion me getting help for myself."

WHAT FOLLOWED...

If Moon was distracted by the domestic incident, the fallout certainly wasn't evident in his play on the gridiron. While awaiting trial, Moon played in all 16 games for the Vikings in the 1995 season. He led the league with 377 pass completions and also matched a career high with 33 passing touchdowns. Moon was named to the Pro Bowl for the eighth year in a row. Unfortunately for Minnesota, the Vikings dropped their final two games of the year to finish at 8-8, missing the playoffs for the first time in four seasons.

Moon's eight-day trial began in February 1996. Felicia Moon testified that she had argued with her husband over financial matters, throwing a candleholder at him. As she begged prosecutors to abandon the case, she testified that her wounds came as a result of Warren Moon trying to restrain her.

The family finally gained closure on February 23, 1996, when Moon was acquitted on all charges. A jury delivered its verdict after less than half an hour of deliberations. Moon thanked the Lord as he spoke to reporters gathered outside the Fort Bend County Courthouse in Texas.

Moon signed with Seattle as a free agent in 1997. At 41 years old, he earned another Pro Bowl selection and set a team record with 3,678 passing yards. After two years with the Seahawks, he had a brief stint with the Kansas City Chiefs as their backup quarterback before retiring in 2000. At the time Moon hung up his cleats, he was the NFL's third all-time leader in career passing yards (49,325) and fourth in passing touchdowns (291).

In July 2008, Moon pleaded guilty to a charge of negligent driving – a reduced charge stemming from an arrest for DUI on December 28 of the previous year. He was sentenced to 40 hours of community service, fined $350, and ordered to attend drug and awareness classes.

Moon co-wrote "Never Give Up On Your Dreams: My Journey" with Don Yeager in 2009, chronicling his life, football career, and personal struggles.

"One of the goals for myself had always been not to get arrested in my life for anything."

MICHAEL IRVIN

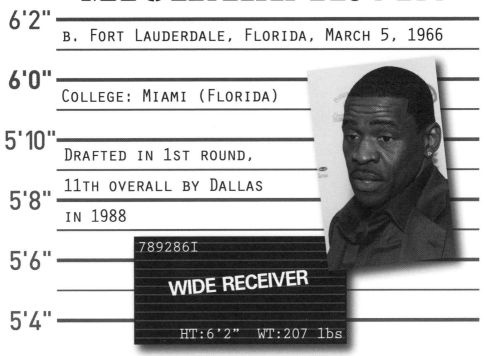

6'2" — B. Fort Lauderdale, Florida, March 5, 1966

6'0" — College: Miami (Florida)

5'10" — Drafted in 1st round,

11th overall by Dallas

5'8" — in 1988

7892861

WIDE RECEIVER

5'6"

5'4" — HT:6'2" WT:207 lbs

IN THE BEGINNING...

Michael Irvin was one of the most prolific receivers in the NFL during his 12-year playing career that eventually ended with his enshrinement into the Pro Football Hall of Fame in Canton, Ohio. Irvin capped his spectacular college days at the end of the 1987 season by winning the Orange Bowl and a national championship under Miami Hurricanes coach Jimmy Johnson.

The Dallas Cowboys immediately inserted Irvin into their starting lineup after making him a first-round selection in the 1988 draft. In that year's season opener against Pittsburgh, Irvin caught three passes, including a 35-yard touchdown strike from quarterback Steve Pelleur, a foreshadowing of Irvin's rise to prominence. His rookie NFL year ended with 654 receiving yards. Irvin's average of 20.4 yards per catch ranked him third-highest in the league in that category, but Dallas limped to a 3-13 finish, the Cowboys' worst showing since their inaugural 1960 season when they went winless in 12 games.

In 1989 the struggling team hired Irvin's old college coach Jimmy Johnson. The on-field results worsened as the team won just once in 16 games. However, better times were looming on the horizon for the rebuilding franchise. Rookie quarterback Troy Aikman evolved into the cornerstone of the offense. A block-buster trade of Herschel Walker to the Minnesota Vikings landed several high draft picks for Dallas, one of which the team used to select running back Emmitt Smith in 1990.

Within a relatively short span, the Cowboys shook off their label as laughing-stocks to regain their moniker as "America's Team." Irvin led the league with 1,523 receiving yards in 1991 – his fourth pro season – and also earned the first of five consecutive Pro Bowl selections. Between 1992 and 1995, Dallas's high-powered trio of future Hall of Fame players Aikman, Smith, and Irvin captured three Super Bowl titles in four years.

As the storied franchise returned to glory, their superstars appeared to be invincible.

THE CRIME...

Irvin was out celebrating his 30th birthday at the Residence Inn in Irving, Texas on March 3, 1996. As told to *Sports Illustrated* by officer Matt Drumm, police officers were called to his room after receiving noise complaints. When they arrived, they found Irvin in the room with his business partner (and former team-mate) Alfredo Roberts, as well as two women in their early twenties described as 'self-employed models.' Scattered among the room were three ounces of marijuana and two ounces of cocaine, plus assorted drug paraphernalia.

One of the women – Angela Renee Beck – claimed to own all of the drugs. All four of the room occupants were booked, but Beck was the only one who was held in jail overnight.

One of the league's all-time greats, Irvin retired at the end of the 1999 season as the ninth-leading receiver in both receptions (750) and receiving yards (11,904).

The Dallas County prosecutor was incredulous at the suggestion that Beck was the sole owner of the banned substances. "It is very difficult for me to believe, based on the circumstances—the amount of marijuana smoke that came out the door, the drugs scattered in different locations throughout the split-level room— that all of this belonged to one person," he said.

As the investigation continued, police said that Beck was having a relationship with Irvin, a married man with two children. She was previously employed at a topless bar that was frequented by Cowboys players.

Prostitution charges were never filed, but Irvin was indicted by a grand jury on one felony charge of cocaine possession and one misdemeanour charge of marijuana possession. He was freed on a $5,500 bond.

WHAT FOLLOWED...

The case went to trial four months later. Prosecutors said that Beck was an unsuspecting pawn who had no knowledge of the drugs that were found in her gym bag on the night of the police raid. Irvin's lawyer, Royce West, countered by asking the jury to question the credibility of the exotic dancers who were scheduled to give testimony in the case.

Irvin pleaded no contest to the felony charge. He received four years' probation and a $10,000 fine as a result of the trial. The misdemeanour charge was dismissed.

Did You Know...?

Irvin's arrest and subsequent trial took a pair of bizarre twists. One led to the revelation of the existence of a drug-ridden bawdy house. The other put his life in jeopardy.

As headlines of Irvin's alleged drug use surfaced, a two-story brown-brick estate near the Cowboys' practice facility became of interest to police. It was rented under the name of receiver Alvin Harper and was infamously dubbed "The White House."

During the Cowboys' championship years of the 1990s, the house became a haven for players to indulge in illicit activities. It was all but impossible to believe offensive lineman Nate Newton's denials of allegations of prostitution and drug use that reportedly took place within those four walls.

On a more frightening note, a Dallas policeman named Johnnie Hernandez was charged with soliciting Irvin's murder. The arrest came amidst accusations that Irvin had threatened Rachelle Smith, Hernandez's common-law wife who also a dancer at the same club where Andrea Renee Beck worked. The threats allegedly came after Smith gave damaging testimony to a grand jury against Irvin, saying that she had visited the same Irving hotel with the football star many times.

Hernandez was arrested after he gave $2,960 to an undercover Drug Enforcement Administration agent who was posing as a killer for hire. As part of a plea agreement, Hernandez accepted a charge of attempted solicitation of capital murder and was sentenced to six years in prison.

The terms of Irvin's probation included 800 hours of community service. In addition, the NFL suspended him for the first five games of the 1996 season.

One of the league's all-time greats, Irvin retired at the end of the 1999 season as the ninth-leading receiver in both receptions (750) and receiving yards (11,904). Although he became a Hall of Fame member in 2007 – his third year of eligibility – critics feel that he may have been inducted sooner if not for his off-field issues. Two years earlier, in 2005, he was charged with drug paraphernalia possession during a traffic stop in Plano, Texas.

BYRON "BAM" MORRIS

6'2"

B. COOPER, TEXAS, JANUARY 13, 1972

6'0"

COLLEGE: TEXAS TECH

5'10"

DRAFTED IN 3RD ROUND,

91ST OVERALL BY

5'8"

PITTSBURGH IN 1994

5'6"

091281M

RUNNING BACK

5'4"

HT:6' WT:244 lbs

IN THE BEGINNING...

Byron "Bam" Morris was the youngest of ten children born to a church deacon and was one of the best rushers in the history of his Class 2A high school. He turned heads during the 1993 season at Texas Tech when he won the Doak Walker Award as the best running back in college football. His rushing total of 1,752 yards set a Southwest Conference record that had been previously held by future Pro Football Hall of Fame player Earl Campbell.

Morris's rookie season with the Pittsburgh Steelers – the team that selected him in the third round of the 1994 draft – turned out to be the most productive of his six-year NFL career. He rushed for 836 yards and seven touchdowns. With Barry Foster entrenched as Pittsburgh's starting running back, Morris saw limited action in the playoffs as the Steelers advanced to the AFC championship game.

The following year was a return to glory for the storied franchise. Pittsburgh

Did You Know…?

Two years after his last day in prison, Morris attempted an NFL comeback. His first choice would have been to sign with the team that drafted him.

"If the Steelers would want to sign me, they wouldn't have to even buy me a plane ticket to get there. I'd drive," said Morris in 2006. "I don't want any favours, no special treatment. I'm not asking for hand-me-downs because I know I won't get it. If people say, 'You don't have it,' I can live with it."

While awaiting a decision from the NFL on his reinstatement request, Morris played in Texas for the Katy Cooperheads of the National Indoor Football League, a team based twenty miles west of Houston. Morris earned $300 per game, a miniscule fraction of the $1.2 million annual salary that he enjoyed at the pinnacle of his professional career.

In the end, Morris's return to the big show never came to pass.

made its first Super Bowl appearance since clinching its fourth championship in 1979, the final hurrah in what was a dynastic decade. In the final quarter, Morris scampered for a touchdown to get his team to within a field goal. But Dallas Cowboys superstar running back Emmitt Smith answered right back to score the final points of the game. Troy Aikman and "America's Team" were triumphant in a 27-17 victory.

Super Bowl XXX was Morris's final game as a member of the Steelers. Legal troubles began to catch up with the fleet-footed rusher. He was waived by the team for violating the league's substance-abuse policy and wound up in Baltimore where he played for two seasons. He also spent time in Chicago and Kansas City before seeing his NFL playing days come to an end.

THE CRIME…

In March 1996, Morris was vacationing in Texas, on the coast of the Gulf of Mexico. As he drove his Mercedes with a friend to Dallas following his holiday, he was pulled over after a policeman noticed him swerving. A search resulted in the officer discovering six pounds of marijuana wrapped in cellophane in Morris's trunk. A gram of cocaine was hidden under the ashtray. Morris pleaded guilty to one count of felony possession in a Rockwell County court. He was fined $7,000 and sentenced to 200 hours of community service and six years' probation.

Following his release from the Steelers, Morris signed a two-year, $1.8 million deal with the Ravens. The NFL assessed a five-game suspension at the start of the 1996 season for the drug crime. While he led the AFC in rushing in the second half of the campaign, Morris soon made headlines again for all the wrong reasons.

In January 1997 he tested positive for alcohol, which was a violation of his probation. The league suspended him for the first four games of the 1997 season. Meanwhile, in Rockwell County, a judge sentenced him to 120 days in jail for the infraction.

Morris's 1998 stint with the Kansas City Chiefs was his most damaging one personally, largely due to the company that he kept. One of his best friends on the team was kick return specialist Tamarick Vanover, who was allegedly connected to drug dealers and was the subject of a federal investigation. Prosecutors alleged that

---

"I was at the top, and it seemed like in the blink of an eye, I hit rock bottom."

Vanover was the leader of a drug ring "hatched at Arrowhead Stadium" – as reported by the *Associated Press*. As part of a plea arrangement in which he confessed to auto theft, Vanover provided grand jury testimony against Morris.

In August 2000, prior to going to trial, Morris pleaded guilty to attempting to distribute more than 100 kilograms of marijuana between January 1, 1998 and May 10, 2000. He was sentenced to 30 months in federal prison. To compound matters, the offence was a violation of his Rockwell County probation. He was given another ten years to serve in Texas state prison at the conclusion of his federal term.

He was eventually released from the Wynne Unit in Huntsville on July 31, 2004.

WHAT FOLLOWED...

Morris sent a handwritten letter to NFL Commissioner Paul Tagliabue just shortly before being granted his freedom. "I don't want anybody to have to go through what I've gone through," Morris told the *Houston Chronicle*. "I was at the top, and it seemed like in the blink of an eye, I hit rock bottom. I hope to talk to kids, starting with 10-year-olds and working my way up to NFL players."

"Looking back, I think going to prison was good for me," Morris said. "State prison got my mind right. I really believe that if I hadn't come to prison, I'd probably be dead because I was living too fast and trying to do too much."

In 2012, Morris was inducted into the Texas Tech Athletic Hall of Fame.

EUGENE ROBINSON

6'2"

B. HARTFORD, CONNECTICUT, MAY 28, 1963

6'0"

COLLEGE: COLGATE

5'10"

UNDRAFTED. SIGNED AS A

FREE AGENT BY SEATTLE

5'8"

IN 1985.

424676R

FREE SAFETY

5'6"

5'4"

HT:6'1"   WT:200 lbs

IN THE BEGINNING…

Eugene Robinson was a three-time Pro Bowler during his 16-year NFL career. He had already been retired for thirteen years by the end of the 2013 season but still ranked tied for 12th all-time in career interceptions (57) with four players. His early playing days, however, made him as much of a longshot to make the professional leagues as the title character in the movie "Rudy." While attending Weaver High School in Hartford, Robinson was just 5'9" and weighed 145 pounds, hardly imposing. Yet he forged his high school career by hitting – even knocking out – opponents much larger than him.

Despite building his reputation at Weaver, Robinson couldn't catch the attention of college scouts, at least not at the schools where football mattered. He attended Colgate University in Hamilton, New York, an institution that prioritized academics over sports and which, as a result, produced few NFL-calibre players.

With Robinson on the roster, however, Colgate made two Division I-AA playoff appearances. The fierce tackle, meanwhile, grew to six-feet and put on another 30 pounds.

Robinson was drafted by the New Jersey Generals of the upstart United States Football League in 1985, but he opted instead to try out for the Seattle Seahawks. The gamble paid off. Although he spent much of his rookie season coming off the bench, Robinson earned a starting job for all 16 games the following year. It was a role he would not relinquish for the next decade. By the first half of the 1990s, Robinson was the Seahawks' most dominant defensive player. He made the Pro Bowl in 1992 and 1993, leading the NFL with nine interceptions in the latter year.

Salary cap issues caught up with the team, and Robinson and his $1 million contract were traded to Green Bay in 1996. His first year with the Packers ended with a Super Bowl victory as Brett Favre led the team to a 35-21 win over New England. Green Bay also made it to the big game the next year where the Pack lost to Denver.

Robinson signed with the Atlanta Falcons in 1998. The team upset the 15-1 Minnesota Vikings in the NFC championship game, but it was on the eve of Robinson's third consecutive Super Bowl appearance that his moment of infamy came.

 THE CRIME...

The stage of Super Bowl XXXIII was Miami, Florida. The Falcons were attempting to deny the Denver Broncos their second consecutive championship. Atlanta was coached by Dan Reeves, who, coincidentally, was at the reins in the Mile High City for three Broncos Super Bowl losses in the 1980s.

The day before the big game, Robinson was arrested on a charge of soliciting a prostitute. According to the police report, he was driving on Biscayne Boulevard, in a seedy area of Miami which was known to attract drug dealers and prostitutes.

"While conducting an undercover prostitution sting, defendant drove up ... and offered the officer $40 for [oral sex]," the police report said, according to *Sports Illustrated*.

"I truly love my wife. I love my kids. I'm sorry that I had to drag them through that type of deal. I'm sorry that it even happened."

The charge shocked Robinson's family and friends. Earlier in the day, he was named winner of the Bart Starr Award, an accolade presented by a Christian organization named Athletes in Action. The award recognizes the player with the highest moral character. Robinson, a staunchly religious man, was married with two children.

Following his booking and release, Robinson had a nearly sleepless night, and it showed on the gridiron, on the game's biggest stage. With Atlanta already trailing 10-3 in the Super Bowl, Robinson surrendered a long touchdown to Broncos receiver Rod Smith on an 80-yard pass from John Elway. Denver won handily, 34-19, as Elway took Most Valuable Player honours in what turned out to be the final game of his Hall of Fame career.

WHAT FOLLOWED...

While the arrest was wildly out of character for Robinson, his Falcons teammates said they were not surprised by the incident, if for no other reason than they had visited the same area of Miami, with similar intentions.

"Guys had been going there all week. It's just that Eugene was the only one who got caught," one anonymous player told the *New York Times*. The charges against Robinson were dropped after he agreed to participate in an AIDS awareness program. He also returned his Bart Starr Award.

"Reputation, I can deal with that. But my wife, that means much more to me. I truly love my wife. I love my kids. I'm sorry that I had to drag them through that type of deal. I'm sorry that it even happened," Robinson said.

Did You Know...?

Robinson had faced Elway many times as AFC West rivals; the defender, playing for Seattle, staring down the future Hall of Fame quarterback of Denver. Given that the teams faced each other twice a year in divisional games, both players had gotten to know each other well.

Elway's touchdown pass to Smith in which Robinson was the targeted defender was, in a way, redemption for one memorable play in the previous year's Super Bowl.

Super Bowl XXXII pitted Denver against Green Bay, Robinson playing in what would be his final game as a Packer. The game lived up to its marquee value as Brett Favre looked to quarterback his team to a second consecutive championship and deny Elway the first championship of his storied career.

Denver pulled ahead 24-17 late in the third quarter. Much to Elway's delight, the Packers fumbled the ensuing kickoff at their own 22-yard line. However, the Broncos quarterback made an ill-fated decision on the very next play when Denver took possession. Despite having the NFL's Most Valuable Player Terrell Davis in the backfield, Elway elected to pass instead of customarily handing off the ball to Davis on a first-down run. Elway's attempt to thread the needle to Rod Smith was promptly intercepted by Robinson two yards into the end zone. The Packers got the ball back, and Favre took the team the length of the field to tie the game.

In the end, it didn't matter. Davis's third touchdown of the evening held up as the game-winner in a 31-24 barn-burner. But Elway surrendered a good chance to put the Broncos up by 14 points and give his team some breathing room. While the decision was inconsequential in Elway's acceptance of the Vince Lombardi Trophy, it showed that even the greatest quarterbacks can sometimes get a little greedy.

RAE CARRUTH

6'2"

B. SACRAMENTO, CALIFORNIA, JANUARY 20, 1974

6'0"

COLLEGE: COLORADO

5'10"

DRAFTED IN 1ST ROUND,

27TH OVERALL BY

5'8"

CAROLINA IN 1997

711509C

5'6"

WIDE RECEIVER

5'4"

HT:5'11"   WT:194 lbs

IN THE BEGINNING...

After graduating from Valley High School in Sacramento, Rae Carruth enjoyed a four-year college career with the University of Colorado Buffaloes where he caught passes from future pro quarterbacks Kordell Stewart (Pittsburgh, Chicago, and Baltimore) and Koy Detmer (Philadelphia). Carruth was named a first-team All-American in his senior year of 1996.

The Carolina Panthers signed Carruth to a four-year deal worth $3.7 million after making him a first-round selection in the 1997 draft. He made an impression in his rookie season, starting in 14 of the team's 16 games and catching 44 passes for 545 yards, leading all freshman receivers in both categories. His performance earned him a spot at wide receiver on the NFL All-Rookie Team.

Carruth broke his right foot in the first game of the 1998 season against the Atlanta Falcons. The injury curtailed his entire year, and he managed to make only one appearance. He suited up for the Panthers' first five games in 1999. The last of those outings came on October 17 against the San Francisco 49ers in which Carruth suffered a sprained ankle that sent him to the sidelines. Carolina hung on for a 31-29 victory, but Carruth caught just one pass for 13 yards. It turned out to be the final game of his NFL career.

Off the field, Carruth was a womanizer. He lost a paternity suit in 1997 and was ordered to pay $3,500 a month in child support payments as a result. Carruth started dating Cherica Adams, a 24-year-old exotic dancer, though the relationship was not exclusive. Adams became pregnant with their son. He asked her to have an abortion, but she refused. Adams confided in other friends that Carruth became more distant following his ankle injury.

 THE CRIME...

On November 15, 1999, Carruth and Adams met for a movie date. It was only the second time they had seen each other since Adams revealed her pregnancy. After the movie, they left the cinema in South Charlotte in separate cars, Carruth driving in front of Adams. Shortly after midnight, a car drove beside Adams where one of its occupants fired a gun directly at her. Adams was struck with four bullets in her back.

Despite the excruciating pain, Adams summoned the strength to call 911. She described her situation to the dispatcher, and speculated that Carruth was involved in the shooting. She also explained that she was seven months pregnant. After the shots were fired, Carruth fled the scene.

When police arrived, they found only Adams, bleeding and clinging to life. She was rushed to Carolina's Medical Center where doctors were able to save her baby boy, named Chancellor Lee, via an emergency C-section. While in hospital Adams – in critical condition – wrote handwritten notes in which she described the night's horrific events. She said Carruth stopped his vehicle in front in order

Did You Know...?

The television program "Law And Order" based an entire episode of its series on the headlines surrounding the Carruth case. Episode 14 of Season 11 is titled "A Losing Season." A basketball player was substituted for a football player. The plot has Detectives Lonnie Briscoe (played by Jerry Orbach) and Ed Green (played by Jesse L. Martin) investigating the fiancé of a pregnant woman who is found dead in the trunk of her car.

A professional basketball player named Chris Cody (played by Kevin Daniels) becomes the prime suspect. As the episode plays out, the baby survives while the star athlete's unwillingness to pay child support payments becomes the motive in the killing.

After Daniel's character Cody is convicted, a memorable exchange takes place between District Attorneys Jack McCoy (Sam Waterson) and Abbie Carmichael (Angie Harmon):

McCoy says: "A man murders the mother of his baby to avoid child support, and he ends up paying for the rest of his life." To which Carmichael replies "A losing season, all the way around."

to block her, just before the drive-by shooting occured.

Carruth was arrested along with three other suspects and charged with conspiracy to commit murder and also attempted murder. He pledged a $3 million bond under the condition that he would surrender to police if either Adams, or their son, died. When Adams died on December 14, the charges were upgraded to first-degree murder.

Instead of turning himself in as agreed, Carruth fled the Tar Heel State. He was eventually discovered by FBI agents hiding in the trunk of a friend's car in Wildersville, Tennessee.

WHAT FOLLOWED…

The trial began on October 23, 2000. The prosecutors' case was based on the premise that Carruth did not want to pay child support. In particular, Carruth was already under such an obligation, and his football injuries had placed his career in jeopardy.

The Charlotte Observer reported that several witnesses testified against Carruth, saying that he opted to arrange to have Adams killed after his first plan failed, which was "to have her beaten up so she would have a miscarriage."

Two of Carruth's co-defendants also gave testimony damning Carruth, as did two ex-girlfriends, one of whom said that he, "confessed involvement in the shooting as they waited at the hospital."

The jury deliberated for over 18 hours over four days. Incredibly, Carruth was found not guilty of first-degree murder, escaping the death penalty. He was convicted of the conspiracy charge, shooting into an occupied vehicle, and using an instrument to attempt to kill an unborn child. On January 22, 2001, he was sentenced to 18-24 years in prison.

Chancellor Lee, who survived the shooting despite being born ten weeks premature, went into the custody of Saundra Adams, Cherica's mother. Chancellor was inflicted with cerebral palsy and showed symptoms of the ailment in his infancy. But Saundra Adams found inspiration in her grandson. "He is our miracle child. He's got such a strong will, just like his mom," she said.

Bill Polian, the general manger who drafted Carruth reflected on the case in January 2014. "It was really difficult," Polian told the *New York Daily News*. "We had no inkling there was anything like this in his future. We did pretty extensive research on him. It was pretty shocking. You feel terrible for the young lady, the child, and, of course, Rae."

RAY LEWIS

6'2"

B. BARTOW, FLORIDA, MAY 15, 1975

6'0"

COLLEGE: MIAMI (FLORIDA)

5'10"

DRAFTED IN 1ST ROUND,

26TH OVERALL BY

5'8"

BALTIMORE IN 1996

614245L

5'6"

LINEBACKER

5'4"

HT:6'1" WT:245 lbs

IN THE BEGINNING…

A standout with the University of Miami Hurricanes, Ray Lewis was the second ever draft pick in the history of the Baltimore Ravens, which had been relocated from Cleveland in 1996. He inked a five-year deal with a $1.3 million signing bonus in July, prior to the start of the opening of training camp. The rookie didn't disappoint in the first game of the team's new incarnation, recording seven tackles and an interception in the Ravens' season-opening win.

Lewis quickly established himself as a defensive stalwart in the NFL. He led the league with 210 tackles in his sophomore year of 1997 and was named to the first of five consecutive Pro Bowl games. The following year, he signed a four-year, $26 million contract extension, making him the highest-paid middle linebacker in the league.

The Ravens changed coaches in 1999, bringing in Brian Billick to replace Ted

Marchibroda. It was the beginning of a strong mentorship as Billick challenged Lewis to achieve even greater excellence. By the end of the 16-game campaign, Lewis was once again the NFL's leader with 198 tackles. More importantly for the team, Baltimore finished with an 8-8 record, the first non-losing mark in franchise history.

Super Bowl XXXIV was played in Atlanta between the St. Louis Rams and Tennessee Titans. The Rams were victorious 23-16, a victory that was preserved by Rams linebacker Mike Jones who brought down Titans wide receiver Kevin Dyson at the one-yard line on the final play of the game. Following the win, Lewis and some friends attended numerous Super Bowl parties, one of which produced dire results.

 THE CRIME...

Lewis and friends Joseph Sweeting and Reginald Oakley arrived at the Cobalt Lounge in Atlanta. Also in attendance – in a different group – were Richard Lollar and Jacinth Baker, two friends who had moved to Georgia from Akron, Ohio. At about 3:30am, Lewis's group walked to their rented limousine. Along the way, Sweeting and Oakley got into an altercation with the group that included Lollar and Baker.

Oakley was hit in the head with a champagne bottle, precipitating a huge melee. During the brawl, Lollar and Baker were stabbed to death. Meanwhile, Lewis and his friends fled the scene in the limousine, the Pro Bowl linebacker instructing his passengers, "Keep your mouths shut, and don't say anything."

Lewis was quickly arrested and appeared in court the next day, February 1, on charges of first-degree murder in the deaths of Lollar and Baker. He was held in custody at Fulton County jail without bail. Less than two weeks later, Oakley and Sweeting surrendered to police. Lewis was freed on a $1 million bond on February 15.

Two days later, Lewis made a prepared statement that was approved by his lawyers:

"First off, I'd just like to say that I'm very sorry about the tragedy that occurred in Atlanta. I mean, my sympathy goes out to the families, the friends of both of the men that died. I know their hearts are broken."

He continued:

"But you've heard it many times before, from my attorneys and from a lot of other people, but now you get to hear it from me. I am innocent...I'm looking forward to the day that all the facts come out, everything is out in front, and my name is cleared."

WHAT FOLLOWED...

In the days leading up to the trial, Baker's blood was found in Lewis's limousine. However, the blood evidence was of limited value, according to legal experts, because all three defendants had already admitted to being at the scene of the murders.

As the prosecution began to present its case on May 23, 2000, critics characterized the efforts led by Fulton County District Attorney Paul Howard as incompetent. On two occasions, prosecutors were cited for two Brady violations – that is, failures to disclose exculpatory evidence to the defence.

Did You Know...?

Lewis's son Ray Lewis III chose to follow in his father's footsteps and enrolled at Miami in the fall of 2013. "I know people are going to expect a lot," Lewis III told the *Associated Press*. "People are going to think a lot. People are going to make assumptions before they even get to know me. But, like I said, if I let that get to me, I wouldn't be playing."

Lewis III did not suit up for the Hurricanes immediately. He was a redshirted freshman for the 2013 season, meaning that his athletic participation was delayed in order to spread out his term of eligibility beyond the normal four-year period.

At Lake Mary Preparatory School in Florida, Lewis III had a stellar career as a running back. In his senior year alone he rushed for 1,898 yards and 20 touchdowns.

On June 5, Lewis pleaded guilty to a misdemeanour charge of obstructing justice and agreed to testify against Oakley and Sweeting. The charges of murder against him were dropped, and he was placed on one year's probation and fined $250,000 by the NFL. Oakley and Sweeting were both acquitted. No one has since been convicted in the killings of Lollar and Baker.

Just under eight months later, Lewis and the Baltimore Ravens were celebrating on the field in Tampa, Florida after handily defeating the New York Giants, 34-7, in Super Bowl XXXV. Lewis made three solo tackles and defended three passes on his way to being named the game's most valuable player. However the publicity surrounding his trial got him bumped from the "I'm going to Disney World" ad campaign in which the Super Bowl MVP customarily stars. Quarterback Trent Dilfer got the offer instead.

Altogether, Lewis finished his career with 13 Pro Bowl selections in 17 seasons. He ended his career on a high note as the Ravens defeated the San Francisco 49ers in Super Bowl XLVII following the 2012 season. But the question marks surrounding the deaths of Lollar and Baker have all but irreparably tarnished his image.

On June 5, Lewis pleaded guilty to a misdemeanour charge of obstructing justice and agreed to testify against Oakley and Sweeting.

FRED LANE

B. NASHVILLE, TENNESSEE,
SEPTEMBER 6, 1975

D. CHARLOTTE, NORTH CAROLINA,
JULY 6, 2000

COLLEGE: LANE

UNDRAFTED. SIGNED AS A FREE
AGENT BY CAROLINA IN 1997.

510900L

RUNNING BACK

HT:5'10" WT:205 lbs

IN THE BEGINNING...

In a span of three years, Fred Lane went from being an unheralded hero in the early days of the Carolina Panthers' franchise to a sad footnote in Charlotte sports history. He attended a small Division II school in Tennessee that was, coincidentally, named Lane College. No team selected him at the 1997 NFL Draft, but Carolina took a chance and signed the running back as a free agent.

In his freshman year, Lane led Carolina with 809 rushing yards, scoring seven touchdowns along the way. "Basically, I thought I was going to be sent home on the first cut," Lane told the *Raleigh News and Observer* in 1997. "I thought they just had me in to be a practice body."

Altogether, Lane racked up 2,001 yards on the ground in three seasons with the Panthers, finding the end zone 13 times. His tenure with the team, however, had its share of setbacks.

"He just got shot because he wouldn't leave me alone. I kept telling him to stop."

Once, he was benched for missing a team flight to Dallas. On another occasion, he grabbed his crotch while celebrating a touchdown against the New York Jets at Giants Stadium and was suspended by the team for one game. Towards the end of his time in Carolina, there were accusations that he had missed or arrived late for several team meetings.

Lane was traded to the Indianapolis Colts in 2000, penciled in to be the backup to running back Edgerrin James.

Lane never lived long enough to play a game for his new team.

 THE CRIME...

Lane, 24, and his wife Deidra, 25, had been having marital troubles. In March 2000, Fred Lane was named in a domestic complaint filed by his spouse. Deidra Lane alleged that her husband snatched a necklace that she was wearing during an argument, causing her to fall. The couple had a five-year-old son from Deidra's previous marriage, and the couple had celebrated the birth of their second child – a daughter – in the final days of June.

One week later, on July 6, 2000, Deidra Lane shot her husband twice with a 12-gauge shotgun; once in the chest, and once in the back of his head. Frantically she called 911 in a dramatic conversation that lasted eleven minutes. "He started choking me," she said on the tape that was released by Charlotte-Mecklenberg police, as reported by CBS News. "He just got shot because he wouldn't leave me alone. I kept telling him to stop."

Did You Know...?

In June 2013, ABC News in Raleigh reported that Deidra Lane, now Deidra Gary, helps run a day camp, the Kiddie Kollege Summer Camp at St. Augustine's University. In a circumstance that many would find difficult to comprehend, she is an assistant to Doris Bullock, who was convicted in 1981 for the second-degree murder of her infant child. Bullock's official title is Assistant Vice President for External Relations in the Office of the President.

When the news leaked, the school only released a statement saying: "The safety and well-being of children in our on-campus programs are our top priorities. St. Augustine's University performs background checks on all employees. Doris Bullock and Deidra Gary serve in administrative roles and provide valuable support. They are exemplary employees and productive members of the community."

Parents were understandably distraught and appalled upon the discovery. But one source with the school maintains that there is no official policy on the hiring of ex-felons.

Fred Lane's keys were found still in the door lock when police arrived at the couple's home. His body was inside the front door, face down in a pool of blood.

The shooting occurred just days after Lane was indicted by a Tennessee grand jury on drug charges stemming from an arrest in March of that year. Following a traffic stop, police discovered 1.3 grams of marijuana in his possession and a .22 calibre assault rifle in the trunk of his car, although the weapons charges were eventually dropped.

Lane's death was the third sports tragedy to occur in Charlotte in an eight-month stretch. In November 1999, Lane's teammate Rae Carruth conspired to have his pregnant girlfriend Cherica Adams murdered, a crime for which he was sentenced to 18-24 years in prison. Two months later, Bobby Phills, a guard playing on the NBA's Charlotte Hornets, was killed in a crash when the Porsche in which he was travelling was driving at excessive speed.

WHAT FOLLOWED...

Deidra Lane was charged with murder. Her lawyers argued that the shooting was in self-defence, portraying Deidra as a battered wife who had endured physical and verbal abuse. Documents filed in court alleged that Fred Lane pushed his wife out of a car, and, in another instance, grabbed her by the throat, lifted her off the ground, and threw her into a sink.

Prosecutors alleged that a $5 million insurance policy was the motive in the killing.

Firearms experts testified that Lane was shot from a distance of not more than eight feet. The first shot, which struck his chest "would cause a loss of consciousness very rapidly, within seconds, certainly less than a minute." The second shot had to have been fired with Deidra standing over Fred's body, casting doubt to her assertion that her husband still threatened her prior to the second shot.

On November 5, 2003, Deidra Lane pleaded guilty to involuntary manslaughter and was sentenced to almost eight years in prison. In handing down the maximum sentence, Judge Timothy Patti ruled that the shooting was premeditated, citing that the second bullet was fired after the first shot had incapacitated her husband.

The judgement was handed down a year after her guilty plea to unrelated charges of conspiracy to commit bank larceny, for which she had served four months in jail and was fined $41,200. She was released from prison on March 3, 2009, after serving almost six years at the Raleigh Correctional Center for Women.

ANDRE RISON

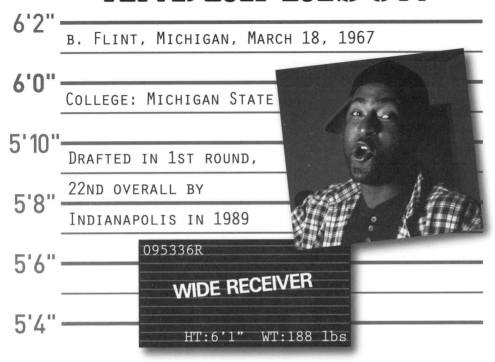

6'2"

B. FLINT, MICHIGAN, MARCH 18, 1967

6'0"

COLLEGE: MICHIGAN STATE

5'10"

DRAFTED IN 1ST ROUND,

22ND OVERALL BY

5'8"

INDIANAPOLIS IN 1989

095336R

5'6"

WIDE RECEIVER

5'4"

HT:6'1"   WT:188 lbs

IN THE BEGINNING...

Over an NFL career that spanned a dozen years, Andre Rison became just as famous for his activities off the football field as he was for his play on the gridiron. A product of the Michigan State Spartans, he garnered the attention of the Indianapolis Colts, who selected him in the first round of the 1989 draft.

At age 22, Rison had a respectable rookie season, starting in 13 games and catching 52 passes for 820 yards including four touchdowns. But his introduction to the pros came with an exuberance of cockiness; he regarded himself to be just as good, if not better than, future Hall of Famer Jerry Rice – widely regarded as the greatest receiver of all-time.

After one year with the Colts, Rison was traded to Atlanta where he enjoyed his greatest success. He was far and away the Falcons' leading receiver in his sophomore year in 1990 with 1,208 yards in the air on 82 catches. His ten receiving touchdowns were second only to the man he had 'chirped' a year earlier, Jerry Rice.

Rison was named a First-Team All-Pro in 1990, and in every year from 1990 to 1993, he was named to the Pro Bowl and finished no worse than second in the league in receiving touchdowns. In 1993, he shared the mark with Rice for most passes caught in the end zone, with 15. Rison set an NFL record with 394 catches over the first five years of his career.

Despite the accolades and awards, Rison is most remembered for his relationship with Lisa "Left Eye" Lopes, a rapper with the R&B group TLC. Their much publicized romance reached a pinnacle of attention on June 9, 1994. As the couple argued in their home, Lopes retreated to a bathroom and set fire to some cardboard in a bathtub. The $2 million estate went up in flames, and Rison lost almost all of his possessions. Lopes was tried for arson. She pleaded guilty, was fined $10,000, put on five years' probation, and ordered to undergo therapy at a halfway house.

 THE CRIME...

Rison was given the nickname "Bad Moon Rison" by ESPN commentator Chris Berman, in reference to the song "Bad Moon Risin'" by Creedence Clearwater Revival. The moniker was well-earned. In September 1993, Rison was arrested for an incident in a supermarket parking lot. He was alleged to have not only hit Lopes but also fired a handgun to ward off a pair of onlookers who tried to break up the fight. Charges were later dropped.

His brushes with the law didn't end there. In 2000, he was waived by the Kansas City Chiefs following a three-year tenure with the team. A week before being cut by the Chiefs, Rison received a non-criminal citation and fined $219.50 for providing a false name to police. He identified himself to an officer as "Brock Middlebrook," but another attending officer immediately recognized the football star.

Rison signed with the Oakland Raiders. During the August pre-season, he was indicted on four charges of passing bad cheques to a jewellery store in 1998 totaling $158,000. The charges came on the heels of accusations that he rented, but did not return, an audio recorder worth $1,100 from a guitar store in Kansas. In both instances, Rison received probation.

Most notoriously, Rison appeared before judges for overdue child support payments. In December 2004, he was jailed after failing to make any of the $3,500 monthly payments owed to Raycoa Handley, the mother of two of his teenage sons, for over two years. Rison spent a month behind bars and was freed only after he made a $10,000 payment. As recently as July 2012, he was put on five years' probation and ordered to pay $300,000 after failing to pay more than $10,000 in child support over a three-year stretch beginning in August 2008, proving that the leopard hadn't changed his spots.

Did You Know...?

Rison is one of only a handful of players to win both a Super Bowl (Green Bay, 1996) and a Grey Cup (Toronto, 2004). However, only one individual has achieved both championships representing the same city.

Linebacker O.J. Brigance began a productive CFL career as a member of the B.C. Lions. He was a two-time West Division All-Star between 1991 and 1993. As the league embarked on an ill-fated experiment to expand into the United States, Brigance joined the Baltimore franchise. The 1995 edition of the squad defeated the Calgary Stampeders to win the Grey Cup.

Brigance then left for the NFL where he signed with the Miami Dolphins. Over four seasons with the club, ending in 1999, he was twice named team captain. He joined the Baltimore Ravens in 2000, earning a championship ring as his team defeated the New York Giants in Super Bowl XXXV.

In 2007, Brigance was stricken with amyotrophic lateral sclerosis (ALS, commonly known as Lou Gehrig's disease). While he can't speak and is confined to a wheelchair, Brigance continues to advocate for research into the disease. In October 2013, he celebrated the release of a new book. "Strength of a Champion: Finding Faith and Fortitude Through Adversity."

With the CFL unlikely to return south of the border, the rare single-city, double championship by Brigance will almost certainly never be repeated.

In December 2004, he was jailed after failing to make any of the $3,500 monthly payments owed to Raycoa Handley, the mother of two of his teenage sons, for over two years.

WHAT FOLLOWED...

Rison didn't start in any of the Raiders' games in 2000, which turned out to be his final NFL season. Tragically, Rison's former girlfriend Lisa Lopes died in an accident in Honduras on April 25, 2002, when the rented SUV that she was driving rolled after Lopes swerved to avoid another vehicle.

In 12 years in the NFL, Rison made close to $20 million in salary and signing bonuses, while finishing among the top of the all-time list with 84 receiving touchdowns (18th, as of the end of the 2013 season).

But because of legal bills and exorbitant spending, his net worth plummeted. His financial fall from grace was detailed in an ESPN "30 for 30" documentary titled "Broke."

JEREMIAH PHARMS

6'2"

B. SACRAMENTO, CALIFORNIA, JUNE 24, 1978

6'0"

COLLEGE: WASHINGTON

5'10"

DRAFTED IN 5TH ROUND,

134TH OVERALL BY

5'8"

CLEVELAND IN 2001

899281P

LINEBACKER

5'6"

5'4"

HT:6' WT:250 lbs

IN THE BEGINNING...

A highly-touted defensive prospect coming out of Sacramento's Valley High School, Jeremiah Pharms made life miserable for opposing quarterbacks with his combination of speed, agility, and brute strength. In his senior year he had two interceptions and eight sacks after which he joined the University of Washington.

Pharms was redshirted in his freshman year of 1996 after breaking his thumb, but by 1999 he had established himself as a regular starter and one of the best tacklers on the Huskies defence.

Pharms made four tackles in the Holiday Bowl against Kansas State, a game that ended in heartbreak for Washington. The Wildcats scored the winning touchdown on a drive that chewed up over nine minutes of the clock in the fourth quarter as Kansas State emerged victorious, 24-20.

The Cleveland Browns selected Pharms in the fifth round of the 2001 draft.

He was offered a three-year contract worth $1 million, but before he could put pen to paper, Pharms had his NFL career snuffed out.

THE CRIME...

Pharms was arrested and charged with a crime that occurred 13 months before his name was called at the NFL draft.

As documented in a *Seattle Times* article on March 14, 2000, Pharms visited the apartment of a Seattle drug dealer named Kerry Sullivan. He bought about an eighth of an ounce of marijuana for $40, then left. About three hours later, one of Sullivan's roommates answered a knock on the door, and two armed intruders entered.

While his roommate was held at gunpoint, Sullivan wrestled with the other interloper – a man wearing a ski mask and carrying an automatic gun. The robber pistol-whipped Sullivan, shot him in the chest, then grabbed a bag of marijuana that had a street value of $1,000 before fleeing into the night.

Pharms was arrested and charged with a crime that occurred 13 months before his name was called at the NFL draft.

When detectives arrived at the crime scene, a witness took them to a white Chrysler LeBaron that had been vacated expeditiously by two men. A bloody fingerprint was found outside the door handle, while inside laid a glove that not only had a blood stain but was clearly identifiable as being part of a football uniform. A roommate of Sullivan's gave police a physical description of the shooter that matched Pharms.

Sullivan survived the shooting, telling investigators that he believed the culprit to be Pharms. The evidence against the football player appeared overwhelming, but the case hit a snag when the lead investigator had difficulty finding the correct address for his suspect. When Pharms's home was finally located, police found fingerprints, a saliva sample, and marijuana pipes, but no drugs.

The prints were quickly matched to the fingerprint on the LeBaron, but a backlog of DNA cases caused a delay in analyzing the saliva sample. By the time the DNA match was confirmed, the 2000 football season was underway and the shooting was six months in the past.

Even with the solid physical evidence, prosecutors were loath to proceed with an arrest. Rightly or wrongly, Pharms had the celebrity status of a football player and the jury would be unsympathetic towards a drug-dealing victim, they reasoned.

Did You Know...?

The 2001 Rose Bowl in which Pharms played capped off a monumental season for the Huskies as they defeated the Purdue Boilermakers, 34-24. Purdue's quarterback was Drew Brees, who was destined for football greatness. Drafted by the San Diego in 2001, Brees played for the Chargers for five years before signing with the New Orleans Saints as a free agent.

Brees has established himself has one of the game's highest-rated passers, leading the league in touchdown passes in four of five seasons between 2008 and 2012. He was named Super Bowl MVP in 2009 as the Saints defeated the Indianapolis Colts to win the NFL championship.

On Washington's side of the gridiron, a *Seattle Times* story published years later revealed that Pharms was hardly the only lawbreaker on the team.

Safety Curtis Williams had an outstanding warrant for assault charges, accused of breaking his wife's arm and nose, and allegedly cutting her face. He had already been convicted and served jail time for choking his spouse.

Tight end Jerramy Stevens was under investigation for rape. Prosecutors eventually decided not to pursue charges.

Incredibly, no fewer than twelve members of the Rose Bowl-winning team were arrested that year.

A month later, in a secret inquiry judge hearing, the lead prosecutor obtained testimony from Pharms's girlfriend who owned the LeBaron. The girlfriend said in the hearing that the LeBaron, which she frequently loaned to Pharms, had been stolen on the night of the robbery. Also, she said Pharms – a married man – smoked marijuana every day.

Pharms played the full 2000 season with the Huskies, earning a trip to the Rose Bowl. He didn't return to his home in Lynnwood, which had been investigated by police after a neighbour tipped off allegations about animal abuse involving four pit bulls. In January, an officer discovered Pharms's wife Franquell loading furniture from the house into a truck. Franquell was informed of a court summons issued to Pharms on the charges related to the dogs.

Her husband didn't return.

WHAT FOLLOWED...

Pharms was arrested on robbery charges on May 1, 2001, and released on $250,000 bail. He was promptly released by the Cleveland Browns. "Our decision to waive Jeremiah Pharms was prompted by our conclusion that this young man must totally dedicate himself to his family and the preparation of his defence," said Browns president and CEO Carmen A. Policy in a statement. "We wish him the best of luck in dealing with these challenges."

Pharms faced as much as 20 years in prison, but he accepted a plea bargain that saw his sentenced reduced to 41 months. The second burglar in the robbery was never identified or arrested.

On a Department of Corrections questionnaire, Pharms wrote, "I was two days away from being a millionaire. And it was taken away because of a mistake."

After his release, Pharms played for two seasons with the New York Dragons of the Arena Football League, ending in 2007.

JEREMIAH PARKER

6'2"

B. FRANKLIN, LOUISIANA, NOVEMBER 15, 1977

6'0"

COLLEGE: CALIFORNIA

(BERKELEY)

5'10"

DRAFTED IN 7TH ROUND,

217TH OVERALL BY NEW YORK

5'8"

GIANTS IN 2000

123654P

5'6"

DEFENSIVE END

5'4"

HT:6'5" WT:250 lbs

IN THE BEGINNING...

Defensive end Jeremiah Parker had a remarkable career at DeAnza High School in Richmond, California. In seven games as a senior, he recorded 87 tackles and seven sacks, while also blocking a punt and recovering a pair of fumbles.

Although Parker was recruited by several colleges, he chose to stay close to home to be near his family. His brother, Theo, was confined to a wheelchair as a result of a drive-by shooting in 1994. Parker attended California and played four seasons as a member of the Golden Bears, largely in the shadow of future San Francisco 49ers first-round pick Andre Carter. Parker's final college game was against rival Stanford on November 20, 1999.

The New York Giants drafted Parker in the seventh round in 2000. With a roster that included future Hall of Famer Michael Strahan and Cedric Jones, the 23-year-old Parker was relegated to the lower rungs of the depth chart. He appeared in only four games – none as a starter – and was used mainly on special teams. Parker was inactive for all three of the team's playoff games as the Giants claimed the NFC championship. They were handily defeated by the Baltimore Ravens in Super Bowl XXXV.

 THE CRIME…

Parker and his girlfriend, 19-year-old Tauleah Kelly, lived in a condominium in Haledon, New Jersey, along with their 4-year-old son, Elijah Kelly. On May 12, 2001, Parker drove Elijah to Wayne General Hospital. Elijah was stabilized before being transferred to St. Joseph's Wayne Hospital where he was placed on life support. Two days later, the young boy died.

Elijah's parents quickly became the focus of a police investigation. Authorities found blunt force trauma around the head along with belt marks and bite marks.

Did You Know…?

Four months before Elijah Kelly's death, Parker gave an interview to the *St. Petersburg Times* in which he described his relationship with his older brother, Theo, who was one year his senior. Theo was 17 years old when he was rendered a quadriplegic after a drive-by shooting. The horrifying incident occurred in front of the family home in Richmond. As Theo was walking to work, he was shot four times by perpetrators who were targeting the neighbours who lived across the street.

Parker was asked if he had any sympathy for Carolina Panthers receiver Rae Carruth, who in 1999 orchestrated a drive-by shooting to kill his pregnant girl-friend who refused to have an abortion. He responded as follows:

"Once you get to this point and you understand how you got to this point, you don't do anything to mess up your life or your money. Do you know a better way to make this kind of money for 17 weeks and live the lifestyle that we live?…Then you deserve what you get."

The eerily prophetic words came back to haunt Parker, the abusive father, in short time.

The prosecutor in Passaic County alleged that Elijah had been shaken in an upstairs bedroom, and also linked the belt marks to Parker.

Parker and Kelly were arrested and charged with aggravated manslaughter, endangering the welfare of a child, and one count each of neglect. They both pleaded not guilty. Parker posted $300,000 bail, using the condominium as collateral.

Andre Carter, Parker's former Golden Bears teammate, was incredulous at hearing the news of the arrest. "Playing with him these three years, he's been like a big brother to me. He's like the sweetest man I know," Carter offered during an interview with the *San Francisco Chronicle*.

Parker's high school assistant coach Jim Kinnison went on to work over three decades in the Almeda County district attorney's office. When asked to comment on the case, Kinnison was understandably torn between defending his protégé, who he knew personally, and upholding his personal integrity as an investigations unit lieutenant who had seen more than his fair share of criminal evidence. "If it's true, Jeremiah has got some real problems," Kinnison said. "I'd have never thought Jeremiah would get involved in something like that — if he did."

"He's not a criminal. Even if he did it, he's not a criminal. I've been around a lot of bad guys for a long time, and I never thought Jeremiah would get into trouble."

The Giants released Parker in June 2001.

WHAT FOLLOWED...

The ensuing trial pitted Parker and Kelly against each other, each alleging that the other was responsible for Elijah's death. Prosecutors contended that Parker repeatedly used a belt or an electrical cord to strike Elijah. Parker was also quoted by investigators as saying that he punished his son by making him stand shivering in front of a fan.

While in jail, Kelly had told the *Herald News* of West Paterson (New Jersey) that she, too, was the victim of Parker's physical abuse. According to Kelly, Parker once poured gasoline over her, lit a match and said "What would you do if I dropped this?" At the trial, court documents also said that Kelly was punched, burned in the face with a cigar, and also nearly suffocated with a pillow, all at the hands of Parker.

"Playing with him these three years, he's been like a big brother to me. He's like the sweetest man I know."

But Parker countered with accusations that Kelly was the aggressor. Parker's lawyer claimed that Kelly disciplined Elijah by sticking him in a refrigerator. On the day that the couple drove Elijah to the hospital, investigators found a child-sized palm print in the couple's refrigerator, which had its shelves removed.

A medical examiner testified that Elijah had sustained injuries that included a broken rib and head trauma, in addition to the belt and bite marks.

Parker was convicted of the child endangerment charge but acquitted on the manslaughter charge. On September 5, 2003, he was handed the maximum sentence of ten years in prison for his role for Elijah's death. He also received a six-month concurrent sentence for marijuana possession. Kelly pleaded guilty in exchange for testimony against Parker. She received a seven-year term in prison.

In July 2007, a New Jersey judge rejected a petition to have Parker's sentence reduced.

MICHAEL PITTMAN

6'2"

B. NEW ORLEANS, LOUISIANA, AUGUST 14, 1975

6'0"

COLLEGE: FRESNO STATE

5'10"

DRAFTED IN 4TH ROUND,

95TH OVERALL BY ARIZONA

5'8"

IN 1998

218666P

5'6"

RUNNING BACK

5'4"

HT:6' WT:218 lbs

IN THE BEGINNING...

In his senior year – 1997 – at Fresno State, Michael Pittman led the Western Athletic Conference with 238 rushing attempts and 270 plays from scrimmage. His total of 1,312 yards from scrimmage was also best in the conference. The Arizona Cardinals, looking to bolster their backfield after finishing last in the 30-team NFL in rushing yards the previous year, acquired Adrian Murrell in a trade with the New York Jets. They also made Pittman a fourth-round selection at the 1998 draft.

Murrell became the team's top rusher with 1,042 yards in 1998 as the Cardinals made the playoffs for the first time in 16 years. Pittman saw little time on the field, carrying the ball just 29 times for 91 yards. Arizona upset the NFC East-leading Dallas Cowboys in an NFC wild card game before losing to Minnesota in the divisional round.

Unfortunately for Arizona fans, the season was a flash in the pan as the team suffered another decade of losing records. The pinnacle of Pittman's time with the Cardinals was the 2001 season in which he started in 14 of the team's 16 games, rushed for 846 yards, and had five touchdowns.

Off the field, Pittman was having domestic issues, with disturbing results.

Did You Know…?

The Tampa Bay team that won the Super Bowl at the conclusion of the 2002 season was coached by Jon Gruden. It was his first season with the Buccaneers after spending the previous four years with the Oakland Raiders – the AFC champions who were handily defeated by Gruden's squad. In February 2002, the Raiders completed a rare transaction by trading coach Gruden to the Buccaneers for $8 million and four draft picks.

Oakland's final game with Gruden as coach will forever be known for a controversial call in which the Raiders lost their 2001 divisional playoff game to the New England Patriots. The now infamous "tuck rule" call spurred the Patriots on the way to a dynasty.

New England quarterback Tom Brady, making his first career playoff start, was leading his team down the field late in the fourth quarter, trailing 13-10. He was hit by Raiders cornerback Charles Woodson and the football squirted loose and was recovered on the ground by Oakland.

The apparent fumble appeared to clinch a Raiders' victory. But referee Walter Coleman cited Rule 3, Section 21, Article 2 of the rulebook: "Any intentional forward movement of [the thrower's] arm starts a forward pass, even if the player loses possession of the ball as he is attempting to tuck it back toward his body."

Thus, Brady's motion deemed the play to be an incomplete pass, and New England retained possession. The Patriots went on to win not only the game but the first of three Super Bowl titles in four years.

After Gruden's departure, the Raiders won the 2002 AFC title but posted a losing record in each of their next seven seasons, winning just 29 of 112 games over that time.

THE CRIME...

Twice in the month of June 2001, Pittman was arrested following disputes with his estranged wife Melissa.

On June 10, Michael Pittman was booked for disorderly conduct. He agreed to babysit their son Mycah when the couple – separated but not divorced – got into a heated argument. Police arrived on the scene after receiving a call from Melissa Pittman. Michael was arrested, but it was finally determined that no physical contact was made, and he was released the next day.

Two weeks later, Pittman was taken into custody again, facing more serious charges. In a fit of jealous rage, he broke a glass door in order to enter Melissa's apartment after seeing his wife with another man through a window. As Pittman faced charges of domestic violence, trespassing and criminal damage, the Cardinals immediately excused him from football related-activities for the summer.

"Michael Pittman has far bigger issues in his life right now than football," head coach Dave McGinnis told the *Associated Press*. "Misconduct on the part of our players is unacceptable. I am furious. Two weeks ago, Michael – eye to eye – assured me he would take care of his personal business. Clearly, he has not."

Pittman was convicted on the domestic violence charge and sentenced to five days in jail and three years' probation. He served two days before being released. He was also suspended by the NFL for Arizona's opening game of the 2001 campaign against Denver under the league's personal conduct policy.

WHAT FOLLOWED...

With a 7-9 record, Arizona failed to make the playoffs, and Pittman's four-year tenure with the Cardinals came to an end. The running back signed with Tampa Bay as a free agent. The Buccaneers inked him to a generous deal worth $8.75 million over five years. Pittman started in 15 of 16 games with his new team, gaining 718 yards on the ground. Saving his best game for the last outing of the 2002 campaign,

Pittman rushed for 124 yards on 29 carries as Tampa Bay demolished the Oakland Raiders 48-21 in Super Bowl XXXVII.

Sadly, the domestic drama between Michael and Melissa Pittman was far from over. On May 31, 2003, Michael Pittman was arrested on six felony counts; three for aggravated assault and three for reckless endangerment. The charges stemmed from an incident in which he reportedly rammed his Hummer into a Mercedes in which Melissa, their son Mycah – now two years old – and their 18-year-old babysitter Kristina Hegland were passengers.

On May 31, 2003, Michael Pittman was arrested on six felony counts; three for aggravated assault and three for reckless endangerment.

Several reports surfaced indicating that, prior to the crash, the couple had argued after Michael Pittman expressed a desire to have Mycah accompany him to the Buccaneers' spring workouts. An additional charge of aggravated domestic violence was added, stemming from the 2001 incidents.

No one was hurt in the crash. Melissa Pittman did not press charges, but the state did. Michael Pittman pleaded guilty to one count of endangerment in exchange for having all of the other charges dropped. He was sentenced to 30 days in jail and was released after serving 14 days. In addition, he was placed on three years of supervised probation and fined $4,500.

Pittman was also suspended for three games without pay by the NFL to open the 2004 season. He returned in Week 4 to start the most productive year of his pro career, rushing for 926 yards in 13 games with seven touchdowns. After six years in Tampa Bay, Pittman played his final season with the Denver Broncos in 2008.

TRAVIS HENRY

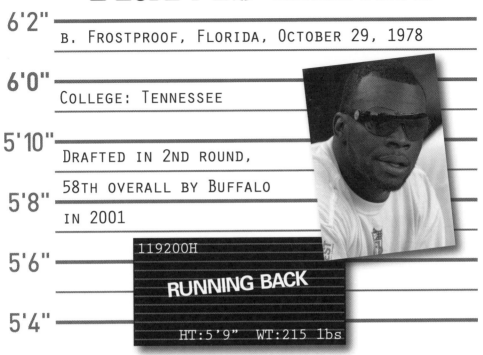

6'2"

B. FROSTPROOF, FLORIDA, OCTOBER 29, 1978

6'0"

COLLEGE: TENNESSEE

5'10"

DRAFTED IN 2ND ROUND,

58TH OVERALL BY BUFFALO

5'8"

IN 2001

5'6"

119200H

RUNNING BACK

5'4"

HT:5'9" WT:215 lbs

IN THE BEGINNING...

In college, Travis Henry was a productive running back with the Tennessee Volunteers, finishing tied for third place in the NCAA's Southeastern Conference with eleven touchdowns and second to Auburn's Rudi Johnson for rushing yards (1,314) and carries (253). Despite being drafted by a sad-sack Buffalo Bills team, his 2001 rookie year saw him earn the mantle as the team's top rusher. Henry gained a respectable 729 yards and produced four touchdowns on the ground. The hapless Bills, however, mired in a quarterback controversy between Rob Johnson and Alex Van Pelt, finished the year with a dismal 3-13 record.

Henry's freshman year didn't pass without legal issues. On October 26, he was charged and accused of attempting to have sex with a 15-year-old girl, who claimed she was nearly 18. He pleaded guilty to misdemeanour sexual conduct and was sentenced to 100 hours of community service.

In his second NFL season, Henry rushed for 1,438 yards – good for fifth place in the league – earning a Pro Bowl selection in the process. He played a total of four seasons in Buffalo and then went to Tennessee for two years. In 2007, the Titans released Henry instead of paying him an $8.3 million roster bonus. He ended up in Denver where he signed a five-year contract worth $22.5 million. His first year with the Broncos was marked by a successful appeal of a one-year NFL suspension for a failed drug test.

But after just one season, Henry was released by Denver coach Mike Shanahan in June 2008, who cited the running back's lack of commitment to the game. Henry continued to work out in the summer, hoping to sign with another team. But there was little interest around the league after reports suggested that Henry was in danger of being suspended by the NFL for a year as a result of a third positive drug test.

It was also discovered that Henry had fathered nine children, all with different women.

THE CRIME...

On September 30, 2008, Henry and an alleged partner James Mack were arrested in Denver after attempting to buy five kilograms of cocaine. The transaction turned out to be a sting operation set up by police. Henry's "dealer" was a drug courier who had agreed to cooperate with Drug Enforcement Administration agents after being caught two weeks earlier near Billings, Montana transporting drugs for Henry and Mack.

According to an affidavit filed in U.S. district court, the courier was a passenger in a car that was stopped by authorities and found to be carrying six pounds each of marijuana and cocaine. The passenger said Henry and Mack supplied him with the contraband that was to be delivered to customers in Billings. As reported by *USA Today*, the courier told the agents that Henry was the "money guy" in a

Did You Know…?

Following his time with the Bills, Henry made two visits to Buffalo as a member of the opposition. One was a Christmas Eve game in 2006 while with Tennessee. The other was the season opener at Ralph Wilson Stadium in 2007 in the backfield for Denver. Although the Broncos won 15-14 on a last-second field goal by Jason Elam, the game is remembered more for a horrifying injury.

As Denver received the second half kickoff, Buffalo tight end Kevin Everett delivered a helmet-to-helmet hit on the Broncos' Domenik Hixon. Everett lay motionless on the ground as medical staff hurriedly scampered onto the field, understanding the gravity of the situation. The game was delayed by fifteen minutes as Everett was rushed in an ambulance to Millard Fillmore Gates hospital where he underwent emergency surgery.

Everett suffered a cervical spine fracture and was temporarily paralyzed. He regained the ability to walk just a few months later. Everett's playing career was over, but reacquiring his mobility following a devastating life-threatening injury was a triumph in itself.

Two days before Christmas, Everett and Hixon – who had since been claimed by the New York Giants after being waived by the Broncos – met for the first time since the on-field collision. "We had a casual conversation," Hixon told the *Buffalo Daily News*. "We talked a little bit about everything."

On February 1, 2008, Everett released his memoir "Standing Tall" in which he chronicled his story and miraculous recovery. Two days later, Hixon was celebrating with his Giants teammates as they upset the New England Patriots in Super Bowl XLII.

drug operation based in the Colorado capital.

The courier owed $40,000 to the operation and had his family, and himself, threatened by Henry regarding the debt. He cooperated accordingly with the agents, leading to Henry's and Mack's arrest. The affidavit stated that Henry broke off a piece of cocaine from the package he and Mack had arranged to retrieve. The cocaine was then cooked as a test to ensure that it was of suitable quality.

The two perpetrators of the alleged crimes were held in federal custody on suspicion of intent to distribute the drug. Henry was released on $400,000 bond, but he was subsequently jailed in May 2009 for violating the terms of his release by consuming alcohol.

On July 15, Henry was handed a three-year prison sentence.

WHAT FOLLOWED...

Henry stated that, at the time his arrest, he was struggling to maintain child support payments to the women with whom he had fathered the nine children. In April 2009, he pleaded guilty to conspiracy to traffic cocaine. On July 15, Henry was handed a three-year prison sentence. He was also given five years' probation and advised to undergo a 500-hour drug treatment program, with the understanding that completion of the program could potentially reduce his sentence by a year.

Henry had faced a ten-year term and a $4-million fine.

"If given the chance, I want to tell kids around the world that using drugs and abusing drugs isn't the way," Henry said as he apologized to the court wearing handcuffs and a prison jump suit.

In August 2012, Henry was reinstated by the NFL. He was free to sign with any of the 32 member clubs as an unrestricted free agent. But, understandably, no one was interested in taking a chance on the former Pro Bowler who was then about to turn 34 years old.

The 2007 campaign turned out to be his final one in his professional career.

ALONZO SPELLMAN

6'2"
B. MOUNT HOLLY, NEW JERSEY, SEPTEMBER 27, 1971

6'0"
COLLEGE: OHIO STATE

5'10"
DRAFTED IN 1ST ROUND,

22ND OVERALL BY CHICAGO
5'8"
IN 1992

287064S

DEFENSIVE END / DEFENSIVE TACKLE

5'6"

5'4"
HT:6'4" WT:287 lbs

IN THE BEGINNING...

Alonzo Spellman played three college seasons with the Ohio State Buckeyes before being selected by the Chicago Bears in the first round of the 1992 draft. At just 20 years of age, he was one of the youngest draft choices in league history.

The Bears signed Spellman to a four-year rookie contract worth $3.06 million. He was groomed gradually by the team instead of being inserted into the lineup right away. It wasn't until his third season, 1994, that Spellman became a defensive starter. He did not disappoint coach Dave Wannstedt, registering 27 tackles, seven sacks, and one interception that year.

By the start of the 1996 season, Spellman had an established pedigree on the gridiron. The Jacksonville Jaguars presented him with an offer sheet of $12 million over four years, but the Bears exercised their right to match any competing bid, keeping Spellman in the Windy City. Buoyed by his team's confidence in him,

Spellman had one of the most productive years of his career with 38 tackles, eight sacks, and two forced fumbles.

But the good times in Chicago slowly began to fade. Spellman missed much of the 1997 campaign with a shoulder injury and was suspended by the team for three games after he refused the club's request to treat the ailment by undergoing arthroscopic surgery. Much more seriously, in March 1998, Spellman was diagnosed with bipolar disorder after an incident in which he threatened to commit suicide while at the home of his publicist.

As described by ESPN.com, Spellman became enraged when informed that the doctor who was scheduled to meet him there to administer a league-mandated steroids test was going to be late. The home was surrounded by police and FBI helicopters as events played out on Chicago's television sets for one and all to see. Former Bears linebacker Mike Singletary drove to the house to rescue his friend without incident and helped him check into a hospital for treatment.

The Bears cut Spellman in June. He missed the 1998 season entirely and became dependent on drugs and alcohol while continuing to be in denial about

Did You Know...?

Spellman isn't the only case of an NFL player being stricken with bipolar disorder. There are parallels between him and Barret Robbins, a former centre with the Oakland Raiders. A veteran of a nine-year career, Robbins was a First Team All-Pro selection in 2002 as the Raiders won the AFC championship, but he abruptly left the team two days before Super Bowl XXXVII, a game in which Oakland was crushed 48-21 by Tampa Bay. A decade later, Robbins said he had been dealing with mental and physical health issues at the time.

Robbins was placed on five years' probation after a January 2005 altercation in which he injured three police officers—and was shot in the process. He pleaded guilty to five charges, including attempted murder.

In 2011, Robbins violated his probation as a result of cocaine possession and served 18 months of a five-year term before being released.

his bipolar condition. The Dallas Cowboys took a chance and signed him as a free agent the following year. After two seasons with the Cowboys, Spellman signed with the Detroit Lions but was cut five games into the 2001 season. Before he could resume his football career, Spellman had another dramatic, terrifying episode.

THE CRIME…

Spellman, his mother Dorothy, and his sister Lorraine boarded a plane – Delta Flight 2038 – on July 23, 2002, a routine flight from Cincinnati to Philadelphia. Before takeoff, Spellman began talking loudly in his seat. His words were incoherent, and he began quoting Bible verses and going off on random tangents. At one point, he made references to airline terrorism, which was a red flag in the wake of the attacks on the World Trade Center just ten months earlier. Nevertheless, the plane took off and the aircraft and its 138 passengers were in the skies en route to Pennsylvania.

When Spellman's ramblings worsened to include profanities, Karen Weaver, a mother of two young children accompanying her, summoned a flight attendant to attempt to diffuse the situation. Spellman only retorted by verbally abusing the attendant with great hostility and then turned his fury to Weaver herself.

"He started criticizing me about the way I looked, the clothes I had on, the type of mother I was," Weaver told the *Philadelphia Daily News*. "I just sat there and took it. He called me a whore, talked about my private parts …and he is YELLING this. The whole plane could hear what he was saying, and at that point I started to cry."

Captain Robert Freund used the aircraft's PA system to implore Spellman to calm down. But Spellman was unyielding, refusing to be silent for any of the passengers or crew who were now having flashbacks of 9/11. When the plane finally landed in Philadelphia, Spellman approached Weaver's husband Steve and said, "I can feel the adrenaline rushing through my hands. I am about to rip your throat out."

Local police were on hand to apprehend Spellman, but under the circumstances, they were fearful for their own safety. "The final outcome could have been disastrous. A man that size, and mentally unstable, would need an army of officers to get him under control," said one police lieutenant. Spellman was eventually taken to a psychiatric hospital in Willingboro, New Jersey, and was arrested by federal agents a week later after creating a disturbance at his brother's home in nearby Mount Holly.

WHAT FOLLOWED...

In January 2003, Spellman pleaded guilty to interfering with the flight crew. He was handed an 18-month prison sentence by Judge Stewart Dalzall, who also made it mandatory for Spellman to take his bipolar medication. "(Those passengers) were scared," Dalzall said to Spellman in handing down the ruling. "And it is unfortunate that that had to happen."

Spellman was released in 2004, having undergone the medical treatment as ordered. He wanted to return to the NFL, but there was no interest from any of the 32 teams. Eventually he found work on the gridiron again, joining the Las Vegas Gladiators of the Arena Football League in 2006.

In January 2008, Spellman led Tulsa, Oklahoma police on a car-chase and had to be subdued with pepper spray bullets. On the resulting charges, Spellman pleaded no contest and sentenced to one year, with immediate release for time served.

In July 2013, Spellman was once again in a courtroom after being charged with making terrorist threats against staff and patients at a Willingboro mental health facility.

DWAYNE GOODRICH

6'2"

B. OAK LAWN, ILLINOIS, MAY 29, 1978

6'0"

COLLEGE: TENNESSEE

5'10"

DRAFTED IN 2ND ROUND,

49TH OVERALL BY DALLAS

5'8"

IN 2000

5'6"

511200G

CORNERBACK

5'4"

HT:5'11"   WT:200 lbs

IN THE BEGINNING…

Before he turned professional, Dwayne Goodrich was an outstanding pass defender with the University of Tennessee Volunteers. In his junior season of 1998, the Vols won the national championship, defeating Florida State, 23-16, in the Fiesta Bowl. During the game that sealed only the second national title in Tennessee's history, Goodrich returned an interception for a 54-yard touchdown and was named the defensive player of the game.

The Dallas Cowboys made Goodrich a second-round selection in the 2000 draft and signed him to a four-year, $1.6 million contract. But the return on the team's investment in their prospect was very low. Goodrich appeared in just five games in his 2000 rookie year – none as a starter – after tearing his hamstring during training camp. A torn Achilles then forced him to miss the entire 2001 campaign.

When he returned the following year, Goodrich started only once in eleven games, making just eight tackles without a single interception. The season ended with the Cowboys posting a third consecutive woeful record of five wins and eleven losses. Goodrich seemed far removed from the celebratory mood at University of Phoenix Stadium in Glendale, Arizona where, almost four years earlier, he had been basking in championship glory.

THE CRIME...

Goodrich and his childhood friend, Bashir Yamini, ventured out for a night on the town on January 13, 2003. Their evening included dinner and a few drinks at a couple of gentlemen's clubs. The men drove in separate vehicles along Interstate 35 with Goodrich – speeding in a BMW – ahead of Yamini.

As he accelerated northbound closely behind an SUV, Goodrich came upon a multi-vehicle accident in which a Mitsubishi was on fire. As the SUV slammed its breaks, Goodrich swerved to avoid it. In the process of trying to manoeuvre past the pileup, he struck three people who were trying to free the driver who had

Did You Know...?

After his release, Goodrich took to speaking engagements at Dallas churches, imploring his listeners not to make the same mistakes that he did. He also was readmitted at age 34 to his alma mater, Tennessee, to study arts and science. His message to his younger classmates was simple: "Don't be me."

Prior to the start of the 2012 training camp, Goodrich visited Cowboys rookie players at the team's practice facility in Valley Ranch to deliver similar warnings. Had third-year defensive tackle Josh Brent been around to hear Goodrich speak, perhaps another tragedy could have been avoided.

In a morbid coincidence, Brent (see page 219) was involved in a fatal car accident that killed Dallas teammate Jerry Brown. Brent was jailed on intoxication manslaughter charges in December 2012.

been trapped inside the car that had its engine engulfed in flames.

One of the victims, 23-year-old Demont Matthews, was propelled some 150 feet along the highway as a result of the impact. He died at the scene. Matthews's childhood friend, Joseph "Joby" Wood, 21, had his head rammed by Goodrich's windshield and succumbed to his injuries in hospital a few hours later. Joshua "Shuki" Josef had his leg shattered.

Goodrich sped away without remaining at the scene of the carnage, fleeing to his home in the Dallas suburb of Coppell. He was found in a state of shock by Yamini, kneeling in his driveway, shaking and mumbling. After consulting with a lawyer, Goodrich was about to turn himself into police when investigators arrived at his door, having traced physical evidence from the accident to his BMW.

"Deep down I probably knew, but my mind wouldn't let me believe that I'd just run over a person. I panicked," said Goodrich in an interview with the *Dallas Observer News* several years later.

WHAT FOLLOWED…

The Cowboys released Goodrich one month after the tragedy. Because Goodrich never took a breathalyzer test after fleeing the scene, charges of driving under the influence of alcohol, or intoxication manslaughter could not be upheld. Goodrich admitted to drinking, but claimed he wasn't drunk when he slammed his BMW into three people.

"I know the perception is that I was drunk," he said. "I'd probably think that, too, if I heard some dude ran over three people. I'd think he was drunk off his ass. But I wasn't."

At his trial, Goodrich testified that he didn't see his victims because his view was obstructed by the SUV that he was following, and that he thought he hit only debris. The prosecuting attorney was unsympathetic. "You panicked because you saw the faces of the men who bounced over your windshield. The men you killed," he said.

Goodrich was convicted by a jury on a charge of negligent homicide, which was a lesser charge than the original indictment of manslaughter. He was sentenced to seven-and-a-half years prison. An additional five-year sentence, to be served consecutively, was also imposed for failing to stop and render aid.

Worsening matters for Goodrich, a Texas law – which has since been amended – removed his eligibility for probation because the negligent homicide charge involved a weapon, the car.

Goodrich was released from prison on parole in October 2011. Five years earlier, civil judgments of $5.3 million and $755,000 were awarded, respectively, to Joby Wood's family and to Shuki Josef. The family of Demont Matthews settled out of court.

Meanwhile, the origin of the first accident from that terrible night in 2003 was traced to Frederick Lamont Person, who was driving the Mitsubishi with a suspended license and open beer cans in the vehicle.

According to the Dallas Police report, it was Person who clipped the back of an 18-wheeler in the right lane of the highway, sending his own vehicle vaulting towards the centre median before coming to rest in the left lane when it caught fire. He was unconscious as Matthews, Wood, and Josef tried to free him from the burning car before they were struck by Goodrich. Person was treated for minor injuries in hospital.

In an effort to deflect some of the culpability, Goodrich's lawyers hired investigators to find Person, who caused the original accident, but to no avail.

LEONARDO CARSON

6'2"

B. MOBILE, ALABAMA, FEBRUARY 11, 1977

6'0"

COLLEGE: AUBURN

5'10"

DRAFTED IN 4TH ROUND,

113TH OVERALL BY SAN

5'8"

DIEGO IN 2000

314305C

5'6"

DEFENSIVE TACKLE

5'4"

HT:6'2" WT:305 lbs

IN THE BEGINNING...

Leonardo Carson impressed his high school football coaches on the defensive line for Shaw High School, graduating to become a pass rusher at Auburn University. His junior year of 1998 saw him return an interception for a 21-yard touchdown. The San Diego Chargers drafted him two years later, but he made just four appearances – all coming off the bench – in his professional rookie season.

Beginning in 2001, Carson started to make his presence felt. Over the next two seasons he started in 20 of the Chargers' 32 games, registering six-and-a-half sacks, 46 tackles, and three fumble recoveries.

Carson's career – and personal life – took a downturn on August 21, 2003. Investigators alleged that on that day, Carson, who had been on leave to attend his grandmother's funeral, broke into the home of Tasha Locke. Locke's sister, Lashaye, and Carson had an eight-year-old daughter together, and Carson had been making threatening phone calls to Tasha, demanding to know the whereabouts of his child. He allegedly broke a window to enter Tasha Locke's apartment, forcibly removing Tasha from the premises and dragging her to his car.

When police eventually apprehended Carson, they charged him with first-degree burglary and second-degree kidnapping. He was released on a $57,500 bond. Chargers coach Marty Schottenheimer refused to comment on the arrest, but San Diego eventually released him from the team on October 14, and he was claimed by Dallas four days later. As a result of the charges, Carson served a 30-day jail sentence in 2004 and was suspended for the opening week of that year's NFL season.

Carson started in all of Dallas's 15 games from Week Two onward as the Cowboys limped to a 6-10 finish. But knee injuries kept him sidelined, and Dallas was forced to cut him in training camp the following year. A brief tryout with the Cincinnati Bengals couldn't resurrect his career, and Carson was eventually forced to retire.

With pro football no longer a staple in Carson's life, the one-time Auburn standout started a business restoring cars, but then he became involved with the wrong people.

THE CRIME...

On April 2, 2009, Carson was arrested on federal drug charges in Dallas. A grand injury indicted him on conspiracy to sell drugs during a four-and-a-half year period from 2004 to 2008. The *Mobile Press-Register* reported that the indictment listed over five kilograms of cocaine, more than 20 grams of crack, and at least 20 kilograms of marijuana in the inventory.

Carson was also charged with aiding and abetting a friend, Kareem Abdul Cook, in the possession with intent to distribute 468 grams of marijuana and 47 grams of crack cocaine. Those accusations stemmed from an arrest on August 19, 2008, in which Cook, along with Carson's half-brother Wilbert, had been arrested after being under surveillance by police. Four vehicles, a pistol, and $1,500

Did You Know...?

Carson's first coach in Dallas was Bill Parcells, the flamboyant, outspoken veteran who spent 22 years on the NFL sidelines between 1983 and 2006, posting a 172-130-1 record over 303 games. His four-year stint with the Cowboys, beginning in 2003, ended a brief four-year retirement.

Although Parcells was already a two-time Super Bowl champion with the New York Giants (1986 and 1990), he couldn't guide Dallas to the playoffs. Along the way, Parcells spent seven seasons in the AFC East division, with four-year and three-year stops with the New England Patriots and New York Jets, respectively.

One of the more offbeat questions that Parcells has had to address was how he earned the nickname "Tuna." He once provided the following answer to the *Milwaukee Sentinel Journal*, citing his first tenure with the Patriots as the team's linebacker coach in 1980:

"There was an old commercial from Starkist with Charlie the Starkist Tuna, so my players were trying to con me on something one time, and I said, 'You must think I'm Charlie the Tuna,' you know, a sucker, and that's kind of how it started. We started with it that year, and they used to wear those little tuna helmets, you know, tuna pictures on their helmets. That's where it all started."

Parcells was inducted into the Pro Football Hall of Fame in 2013.

were seized in the raid, in addition to the drugs.

The case had come under federal jurisdiction because the substances were allegedly transported across state lines, from Texas to Alabama.

WHAT FOLLOWED...

When Leonardo Carson's trial got underway in August 2009, both Cook and Wilbert Carson pleaded guilty and named Leonardo as their supplier.

But testimony from Leonardo Carson's wife, Tonya, suggested that her husband had been set up to take the fall. Arthur Madden, Carson's attorney, emphatically said as much to the jurors.

"Now they're using their association with him to save themselves," he said of Cook and Wilbert Carson. "As they testify here, they've got crushing sentences hanging over them." Throughout the proceedings, defence attorneys attempted to discredit prosecution witnesses, suggesting that they each made deals with the government in exchange for their testimony.

Carson was convicted on four charges, the most serious of which was conspiracy to possess with intent to distribute more than 500 grams of powder cocaine. By the time his sentencing hearing was scheduled, Carson had lost confidence in Madden and requested a new lawyer.

Throughout the proceedings, defence attorneys attempted to discredit prosecution witnesses, suggesting that they each made deals with the government in exchange for their testimony.

"The communication on this is blurred to me. I would like to have more knowledge of what's going on," he explained to Judge Kristi DuBose. Madden was replaced by Robert Ratliff.

On June 10, 2010, Carson was sentenced to ten years plus one month in prison. He had faced as much as 27 years behind bars.

Both Wilbert Carson and Kareem Abdul Cook received reduced sentences of five-and-a-half years and six years, respectively. The allegations of conspiracy plea bargaining to sacrifice Leonardo Carson appeared to be confirmed at Wilbert Carson's sentencing hearing. While family members had jammed the courtroom throughout Leonardo's trial, the stands were empty when Wilbert went before the judge.

JIM McMAHON

6'2"

B. JERSEY CITY, NEW JERSEY, AUGUST 21, 1959

6'0"

COLLEGE: BRIGHAM YOUNG

5'10"

DRAFTED IN 1ST ROUND, 5TH

OVERALL BY CHICAGO IN 1982

5'8"

375322M

5'6"

QUARTERBACK

5'4"

HT:6'1" WT:195 lbs

IN THE BEGINNING…

Outspoken and flamboyant, quarterback Jim McMahon was in the spotlight almost as often for his off-field antics as he was for his throwing arm on the gridiron. After excelling on the football field, basketball court, and baseball diamond at Roy High School in Utah, McMahon attended Brigham Young University, becoming a football star.

Over a stellar four-year college career, McMahon was named the Western Athletic Conference offensive player of the year three times. He led the entire NCAA in passing yards (4,571), completions (284) and attempts (445) in 1980, finishing fifth in voting for the Heisman Trophy.

McMahon's most memorable college game was the 1980 Holiday Bowl when the BYU Cougars faced the Southern Methodist Mustangs. BYU trailed 45-25 with less than four minutes to play, the game seemingly out of reach. But McMahon rallied the team for three straight touchdowns – the last one coming on a 41-yard pass to Clay Brown on the final play of the game – as the Cougars stunned their opponents with a 46-45 win. The game became known as the "Miracle Bowl."

McMahon's talents made him a first-round draft choice of the Chicago Bears, but his rebellious style clashed with the demanding, no-nonsense approach of coach Mike Ditka and NFL Commissioner Pete Rozelle. The quarterback's head-band, for instance, which he wore for the first time during a playoff game, was popular with fans. But the non-traditional fashion statement violated the league's dress code, primarily because it sported the logo of an equipment company. The NFL fined him $5,000 as a result. Nevertheless, the Bears evolved into championship contenders with a roster that included future Hall of Famers Walter Payton, Richard Dent, Mike Singletary, Dan Hampton, and coach Ditka.

Did You Know...?

McMahon was inducted into the College Football Hall of Fame in 1999 and into the Utah Sports Hall of Fame in 2013. Although he has one career Pro Bowl nomination and two Super Bowl rings – one as a starter – McMahon is unlikely to ever get the nod to the Pro Football Hall of Fame.

But what about the BYU Hall of Fame? Surely the engineer of the 1980 Holiday Bowl win and one-time All-American who threw for 84 career touchdowns in a Cougars uniform is enshrined?

Not yet. University rules stipulate that a player must be a graduate to either have his number retired or be honoured into its Hall of Fame. McMahon didn't finish his degree before entering the NFL draft.

However, McMahon enrolled in classes in the fall of 2013 en route to earn his diploma many years after he started. "I was gonna enroll in this math class this fall, but they told me to wait because I might qualify for special-ed math now," he told the *Deseret News*. "I might be able to pass that class — I hope — and then I'll have one other class to do, whatever I want."

McMahon also said he wants to earn his diploma for his father, Jim Sr., who lives in Nevada.

In 1985, Chicago steamrolled over the rest of the NFL to a 15-1 regular-season record, then dominated the playoffs, culminating in a 46-10 win over New England in Super Bowl XX. Throughout the postseason, the Bears gained huge publicity with their video "Super Bowl Shuffle." The team's quarterback showed off his rap skills – or lack thereof – with the line, "I'm the punky QB known as McMahon. When I hit the turf, I got no plan."

The dream season that ended in the Bears' capture of the Vince Lombardi Trophy was the highlight of McMahon's tenure in Chicago. His feuds with Ditka got him traded to San Diego in 1989 after a memorable, yet sometimes tumultuous, seven years in the Windy City.

 THE CRIME...

McMahon played the final eight years of his career for five different teams: San Diego, Philadelphia, Minnesota, Arizona, and Green Bay. He retired after the 1996 season in which he earned a second Super Bowl title backing up Brett Favre with the Packers. McMahon finished his career with 18,148 passing yards and exactly 100 touchdowns to his credit.

In the early hours of November 9, 2003, police in Navarre, Florida were alerted to a pickup truck weaving through traffic and narrowly missing colliding with other vehicles. McMahon, the pickup's driver, swerved across the centre line of a highway before being stopped by a cruiser.

"Don't Be A Punk and Get Drunk."

Police conducted a field test during which McMahon looked at an officer and said, "I'm too drunk; you got me," according to the *Associated Press*. The breathalyzer reading showed that McMahon's blood alcohol level was more than three times Florida's legal limit of .08 percent. The former NFL star was arrested and released after posting a $500 bond. He was charged with drunk driving.

When word of the charges reached the Chicago news outlets, bars in the area – where McMahon still lived – removed posters featuring their local hero that read, "Don't Be A Punk and Get Drunk."

WHAT FOLLOWED...

In June 2004, McMahon pleaded no contest to the charge. He received 12 months' probation and an $850 fine (including court costs) and was ordered to perform 50 hours of community service. His drivers' license was suspended for six months.

Later in life, McMahon faced legal issues of a different sort when he was named in a 2012 lawsuit filed by federal regulators. He was one of seven former board members of a bank sued by the FDIC trying to recuperate $104 million in bad loans. But the Super Bowl champion also struggled with far greater, nearly life-threatening, demons.

The former Pro Bowl quarterback suffered from dementia, brought on by the numerous concussions he suffered while playing football. McMahon was one of several plaintiffs who filed a $765-million lawsuit against the NFL in 2011 alleging that the league concealed the dangers of the medical effects of concussions from its players.

McMahon's health has improved in recent times. In August 2013, he appeared on "The Dan Patrick Show" on Fox Sports Radio saying that, while he still has dementia, he no longer contemplates suicide as he once did. McMahon has also undergone treatment in New York to adjust two vertebrae that were cutting off his spinal fluid, resulting in a backlog of fluid in his brain. The results have been favourable so far.

JAMAL LEWIS

6'2"

B. ATLANTA, GEORGIA, AUGUST 29, 1979

6'0"

COLLEGE: TENNESSEE

5'10"

DRAFTED IN 1ST ROUND,

5TH OVERALL BY

5'8"

BALTIMORE IN 2000

014286L

5'6"

RUNNING BACK

5'4"

HT:5'11"   WT:240 lbs

IN THE BEGINNING...

Fans who flocked to Neyland Stadium at the University of Tennessee to watch Jamal Lewis play could see that the star running back was destined for greatness. The 1997 edition of the team had Peyton Manning at quarterback and Lewis in the backfield, and the pair led the team to an Orange Bowl appearance.

Lewis, a rookie, led the Southeast Conference in both rushing yards (1,364) and attempts (232). The Volunteers went undefeated the following year, claiming the national championship with a win in the Fiesta Bowl. Over a three-year college career, Lewis rushed for 2,677 yards in 27 games, reaching the end zone 17 times on the ground.

Lewis's pedigree made him an easy first-round draft choice by the Baltimore Ravens in 2000. In that season, the freshman started in 13 of 16 regular season games. He capped off a memorable debut by rushing for 102 yards and a touchdown in Super Bowl XXXV as the Ravens ran roughshod over the New York Giants to claim the championship.

In a foreshadowing of future notoriety, Lewis was suspended for four games during the 2001 NFL campaign for a repeat violation of the league's substance-abuse policy. Although Lewis did not miss any games because he was already injured – having suffered a season-ending knee injury – he lost over $230,000 in salary.

The 2003 campaign provided one of the finest offensive outputs by one player in NFL history. Lewis rushed for an unbelievable 2,066 yards, the second-best total of all time (since bettered by Adrian Peterson). He became just the fifth player ever to break the 2,000 yard threshold after O.J. Simpson, Eric Dickerson, Barry Sanders, and Terrell Davis, and since also achieved by Chris Johnson and Peterson. In recognition of his efforts, Lewis was a Pro Bowl selection, a First Team All-Pro, and the Professional Football Writers of America MVP.

In the last outing of that season, Baltimore dueled with the Tennessee Titans in a tight wild card playoff game. Titans kicker Gary Anderson broke the hearts of the Ravens and their fans with a last-minute 46-yard field goal to give Tennessee a 20-17 win.

Because of Tennessee's stifling run defense, Lewis was held to just 35 yards on 14 carries in the playoff loss, which represented a season low. However, less than two months later, he was dealing with a whole slew of other issues.

 THE CRIME…

Federal drug charges were filed against Lewis by an Atlanta grand jury on February 25, 2004. Lewis was indicted on one count of conspiracy to possess cocaine with the intent to distribute. An additional count of using a wireless device was also handed down. The charges stemmed from an alleged incident that took place in June 2000 in which Lewis tried to help a childhood friend

Throughout the ordeal, Lewis steadfastly maintained his innocence.

named Alonso Jackson purchase the drug. The indictment stated that a conversation between Lewis and Jackson also involved a woman, who happened to be an undercover police informant.

Lewis turned himself in to police and pleaded not guilty. He was released on a $500,000 bond. According to an FBI affidavit, a recorded conversation took place in which the informant contacted Lewis on his cell phone to talk about selling the cocaine to Jackson. The two men then met with the woman at a restaurant to go over some further details. About three weeks later, Jackson and the informant met again at a gas station, without Lewis. They discussed drugs, but no purchase was made.

Did You Know...?

Establishing himself as one of the game's greatest superstars, Lewis appeared financially set for life upon retirement. But a lavish lifestyle of exorbitant spending combined with a series of failed real estate investments sent him into bankruptcy. By 2012 he had listed $14.5 million in assets and $10.6 million in debts in a Chapter 11 filing.

One of Lewis's creditors – M&T Bank – bought the naming rights to the Baltimore Ravens' home field. The first game played under the stadium's new name was on September 14, 2003, in Week 2 against the Cleveland Browns. Lewis had a pair of touchdown runs of 82 and 63 yards on the way to setting a single-game record of 295 yards. The mark held for four years before it was trumped by a single yard by Minnesota's Adrian Peterson.

In February 2014, TMZ.com reported that Lewis successfully completed an online financial management course, the Dave Ramsey Education Course.

Jackson was arrested on the same day that Lewis was indicted in 2004.

An additional indictment was issued against Lewis for aiding and abetting Jackson and also for introducing the informant to two other men for the purposes of selling cocaine. Altogether Lewis faced a total of three counts, one for each instance in which he was said to have used his cell phone to broker a cocaine deal.

WHAT FOLLOWED...

Throughout the ordeal, Lewis steadfastly maintained his innocence. He had the full support of the Ravens organization, including head coach Brian Billick.

"I would suggest that you all wait and see what the circumstances are before you rush to judgment or comment because there are some particular circumstances of which I think you'll see why we hold firm to our belief in Jamal," Billick told the *Baltimore Sun*. "You'll see why our support is so strong for Jamal in that this clearly was a 20-year-old young man, a junior in college five years ago, that had a serious lapse in judgment, but not to the degree that people are portending right now."

Lewis and Jackson each faced a minimum of ten years in prison. Taking his usual spot in the Ravens' backfield to start the 2004 season, Lewis played in each of Baltimore's first four games, including a 186-yard performance against Cincinnati in Week 3.

Federal prosecutors offered Lewis a plea deal that included a term of less than one year. He accepted. Lewis was sentenced to four-and-a-half months in jail and served the term during the NFL off-season. He was also suspended for two games for violating the league's substance-abuse policy and performed 500 hours of community service.

SEAN TAYLOR

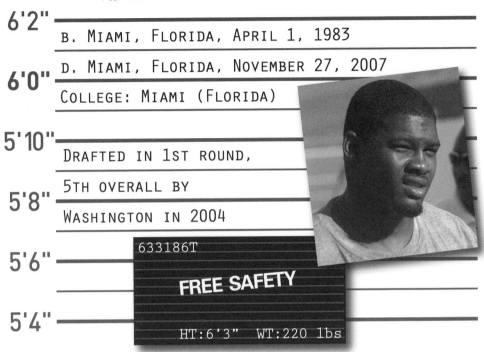

6'2"

B. MIAMI, FLORIDA, APRIL 1, 1983

D. MIAMI, FLORIDA, NOVEMBER 27, 2007

6'0"

COLLEGE: MIAMI (FLORIDA)

5'10"

DRAFTED IN 1ST ROUND,

5TH OVERALL BY

5'8"

WASHINGTON IN 2004

633186T

5'6"

FREE SAFETY

5'4"

HT:6'3" WT:220 lbs

IN THE BEGINNING...

Gulliver Preparatory School is where Sean Taylor first rose to stardom in his hometown of Miami. Attending the affluent high school where students drove luxury cars and were groomed for the Ivy League, Taylor was mainstay in the football team's secondary, helping Gulliver win a state title in 2000.

From there, Taylor stayed close to home to put on the cleats for the University of Miami Hurricanes. The 2002 edition of the team advanced to the Fiesta Bowl, winning 12 consecutive games before losing to Ohio State, 31-24, in a double-overtime nail-biter. For Hurricanes fans, the heartbreaking result ended aspirations of a Bowl Championship Series national title.

The following year, Taylor established himself as the pre-eminent pass defender in the Big East Conference. He led not only the conference, but the entire NCAA, with ten interceptions and three interception returns for touchdowns. The accomplishments made him an All-American and earned him the honour of being the Big East defensive player of the year. Taylor capped off the season with an exclamation point, making an interception in the Orange Bowl as the Hurricanes defeated the rival Florida State Seminoles, 16-14.

After the Washington Redskins chose Taylor fifth overall in the 2004 draft, they put him to work right away, inserting him into the lineup as a starter for 13 of 16 games. The hard-hitting rookie certainly didn't look out of place, making 61 tackles to go along with four interceptions. Washington muddled their way to a 6-10 finish in the first year of legendary coach Joe Gibbs's second tenure with the club.

With a seven-year, $18-million contract in hand, the 21-year-old Taylor was already among the game's elite players, just as he had reached the legal drinking

Did You Know...?

Joe Gibbs was Taylor's coach in each of the late Redskins safety's four professional years. It was the second time around on the sidelines for Gibbs, who had coached Washington between 1981 and 1992, winning three Super Bowls during that stretch.

Gibbs is one of only four coaches in NFL history to hoist the Vince Lombardi Trophy three times, joining Chuck Noll (Pittsburgh), Bill Walsh (San Francisco) and Bill Belichick (New England). But of the four individuals, only Gibbs achieved the feat with three different starting quarterbacks.

Joe Theismann led the way for Washington in Super Bowl XVII. Five years later, it was Doug Williams as the pivot in the Redskins' annihilation of the Denver Broncos. Then, in Super Bowl XXVI, Mark Rypien took MVP honours, quarterbacking Washington to a third championship.

Conversely, Noll, Walsh, and Belichick all benefited from having a current, or future, Hall of Famer at the helm in Terry Bradshaw, Joe Montana, and Tom Brady, respectively. Full credit goes each member of the exclusive list of mentors. However, without having the luxury of a long-time star quarterback, Gibbs deserves at least some mention for being the greatest NFL coach of all-time. He was inducted into the Pro Football Hall of Fame in 1996.

age. He used some of his funds to purchase a pair of new all-terrain vehicles. During one summer night in June 2005, the vehicles were the focal point of an argument in which Taylor's temper got the better of him in a now infamous altercation.

THE CRIME...

Taylor was visiting friends in West Perrine, a high-crime Miami suburban ghetto. As reported in the *Washington Post*, Taylor drove a blue Yukon Denali SUV with a friend, 19-year-old Charles Elwood Caughman, seeking two men whom he had believed had stolen his ATV's. When Taylor located his suspects outside of one home, he got out of his car and, brandishing a gun, pointed the weapon at the pair.

No shots were fired but Taylor and Caughman left the scene only to return ten minutes later accompanied by more friends. According to police, a fight ensued in which Taylor punched 21-year-old Ryan Hill. Meanwhile, Caughman chased down another man with a baseball bat.

Taylor eventually surrendered to police and was released after posting a $16,500 bond. He was charged with two counts of aggravated assault with a firearm – constituting a felony – plus one misdemeanour count of battery. Caughman faced one count of aggravated assault.

Although he faced a maximum of 16 years in prison, Taylor eventually pleaded no contest to two misdemeanour charges. He was placed on 18 months' probation and fined $71,764 by the NFL.

WHAT FOLLOWED...

Although the most damaging incident to Taylor's public image was behind him – at least from a legal perspective – he was also troublesome on the field. In Washington's 2005 wild card playoff game against Tampa Bay, Taylor was ejected for spitting in the face of Buccaneers running back Michael Pittman. Taylor was

On November 26, four armed intruders aged 17 to 20 entered the home in which Taylor lived with his fiancée, Jackie Garcia, and their 18-month-old daughter.

also developing a reputation for delivering late hits and had been fined several times by the league for such infractions.

However, his fierce, physical style of play continued to make him a force on the Redskins' defence. In 2006, he was named to the Pro Bowl, leading the team with 89 tackles.

The first half of the 2007 season, Taylor's fourth in the league, was sensational. Taylor recorded at least one interception in four consecutive games, and he was well on his way to a second straight Pro Bowl selection when he was sidelined with a knee injury in a Veterans' Day game. He never stepped onto a football field again.

On November 26, four armed intruders aged 17 to 20 entered the home in which Taylor lived with his fiancée, Jackie Garcia, and their 18-month-old daughter. Taylor was shot as he attempted to guard the master bedroom that his family occupied. He died the next day. NFL Commissioner Roger Goodell and Reverend Jesse Jackson were among the attendees at his funeral. The Redskins honoured his memory by wearing commemorative patches on their helmets and jerseys with Taylor's number, 21. Taylor earned a posthumous Pro Bowl selection at season's end.

In January 2014, Eric Rivera, Jr. was convicted of Taylor's murder, and was sentenced to 57-and-a-half years in prison. He was 17 at the time of the shooting.

FRED SMOOT

6'2"

B. JACKSON, MISSISSIPPI, APRIL 17, 1979

6'0"

COLLEGE: MISSISSIPPI
STATE

5'10"

DRAFTED IN 2ND ROUND,

45TH OVERALL BY

5'8"

WASHINGTON IN 2001

5'6"

511274S

CORNERBACK

5'4"

HT:5'11" WT:174 lbs

IN THE BEGINNING...

Fred Smoot was a thorn in the side of opposing quarterbacks, making ten interceptions over a two-year career at Mississippi State University. He was named an All-American in 2000. On New Year's Eve, the Bulldogs took to the field in Shreveport, Louisiana, to face the Texas A&M Aggies in the Independence Bowl. In a meteorological anomaly, a blistering snowstorm blanketed the southern state, wreaking havoc with playing conditions. Mississippi State squeaked out a 43-41 overtime win in a game that was dubbed the "Snow Bowl."

Smoot spent the first four years of his pro career with the Washington Redskins, collecting 16 interceptions and three forced fumbles over that time. In the 2005 off-season, the Minnesota Vikings – looking to upgrade their porous defence that was ranked 28th of 32 teams – signed Smoot to a six-year contract worth $34 million. The previous year's edition of the team had finished with a .500 record, losing to Philadelphia in the divisional playoffs.

Minnesota stumbled out of the gate in the 2005 campaign, winning just one of its first four games. The calendar year was already rife with public relations disasters for the team. In March, coach Mike Tice was fined $100,000 for his role in a controversy in which he admitted to scalping part of his allotted Super Bowl ticket quota.

Then, in June, running back Onterrio Smith was suspended for the entire year for a third violation of the NFL's substance-abuse policy. Two months earlier, airport officials found the running back transporting several vials of dried urine, plus a device called "The Whizzinator" – consisting of a fake penis, bladder, and athletic supporter – that was used to beat drug tests.

In Week 4 of the 2005 NFL season, the Vikings suffered a humiliating 30-10 loss to the Atlanta Falcons on the first Sunday in October. Minnesota headed into its bye week hoping to refocus and salvage playoff hopes with three-quarters of the season still remaining. Soon afterwards, the team's sagging image took yet another damaging hit.

 THE CRIME…

Reports surfaced that, on October 6, 2005, a lewd party took place at which as many as 17 Vikings players boarded one of two yachts on Lake Minnetonka. There were allegations of naked lap dancing, oral sex, and excessive drinking on the boats. Investigators tried to confirm suggestions that strippers had been flown in for the event.

Four of the Minnesota players faced charges as a result of the evening's debauchery, which was dubiously nicknamed the "Love Boat" scandal by journalists and late-night talk show hosts alike. Fred Smoot, along with quarterback Daunte Culpepper, tackle Bryant McKinnie, and running back Moe Williams were all charged with misdemeanours, punishable by up to 90 days in jail, and/or a $1,000 fine.

The list of criminal complaints read like the script of an adult film. Culpepper and Williams reportedly received a lap dance from a naked companion, while McKinnie and three of his teammates engaged in oral sex with four different women. Smoot was said to have been using a sex toy with two females.

Four of the Minnesota players faced charges as a result of the evening's debauchery, which was dubiously nicknamed the "Love Boat" scandal by journalists and late-night talk show hosts alike.

The scandal was a public-relations nightmare for the Vikings. It occurred in the relatively low-key state of Minnesota, far removed from the bustling metropolitan areas of either New York or Los Angeles where such ill-reputed activities might well have been more tolerated or ignored by media outlets.

The psychological impact was evident on the gridiron. Any optimism about a potential turnaround coming out of the bye week was snuffed as Minnesota suffered an embarrassing 28-3 defeat to their division rivals, the Chicago Bears. "If I was to say (the controversy) didn't affect us at all, I'd be lying to you," coach Tice told *Sports Illustrated*.

WHAT FOLLOWED…

The four Vikings faced identical charges of indecent conduct, disorderly conduct, and lewd or lascivious conduct.

Charges against Culpepper were dropped because of a lack of probable cause. The Minnesota quarterback had the benefit of a witness, who corroborated

Culpepper's testimony of innocence.

"I was confident when the legal process began that the truth would come out, and I am glad that my innocence has been proven. I greatly appreciate Judge (Kevin) Burke's sensitivity to the damage that can be done to a person's reputation when they are wrongly charged," said Culpepper in a statement.

Williams was fined $300 and ordered to perform 30 hours of community service. Smoot and McKinnie each pleaded guilty and fined $1,000, with orders to complete 48 hours of community service.

Miraculously, the team was able to recover from the fiasco to win eight of its final eleven games and finish with a 9-7 record. But the NFC was too tightly contested for the Vikings to earn a playoff spot, despite the fact they had achieved the feat one year earlier by winning one fewer game.

Did You Know...?

In January 2014, Smoot — more than four years into his retirement — attempted to find a charitable way to transform the image of the event that had gained notoriety around the world.

The NFL alumnus took to the Internet to promote "The Fred Smoot Love Boat, Part Two" with proceeds to benefit the Wounded Warrior Project, an initiative that was created to aid wounded veterans. The event had been scheduled for March 16 to take place on a boat called Cherry Blossom along the Potomac River. The all-you-can-drink party required a minimum of 200 people to sign up before it could take place. But the proposed fundraiser was cancelled when it fell well short of that number.

Speaking to Washington, D.C. radio station 106.7 The Fan, Smoot casually reflected on how he became the fall guy for the "Love Boat" scandal, despite having been with the team for only four regular season games when it had occurred.

"I make the call to the boating company, and they was like, 'Yeah, no problem man, just leave us a credit card,'" Smoot explained. "And guess what I did? I left my credit card in my name. But don't forget, I'm the new guy. I hadn't been a Viking but two months. I was the new guy. I was just learning how they do stuff."

ADAM "PACMAN" JONES

6'2" ——————————————————————
B. ATLANTA, GEORGIA, SEPTEMBER 30, 1983

6'0" ——————————————————————
COLLEGE: WEST VIRGINIA

5'10" ——————————————————————
DRAFTED IN 1ST ROUND,

6TH OVERALL BY
5'8" ——————————————————————
TENNESSEE IN 2005

314286R
5'6" ——————————————————————
PUNT RETURNER /
CORNERBACK
5'4" ——————————————————————
HT:5'11"   WT:187 lbs

IN THE BEGINNING...

His given name is Adam Bernard Jones. But thanks to a childhood propensity to drink milk "with the voraciousness of the Pac-Man video game character" – according to the Tennessee Titans media guide – Jones was given the nickname "Pacman."

Playing for the West Virginia Mountaineers in university, Jones was an effective cornerback who also served as the deep man on punt returns. In three seasons, from 2002-2004, the Mountaineers advanced to one Continental Tire Bowl and two Gator Bowls but ended up on the losing end each time.

A first round draft choice of the Titans in 2005, Jones immediately earned a spot on the starting roster. He averaged 26.2 yards per kickoff return in his freshman campaign to rank fourth in the NFL in that category. The highlight of Jones's season was a 52-yard punt return for a touchdown in Week 13 against the Houston Texans.

Jones's sophomore year of 2006 saw "Pacman" establish himself as an elite player on special teams. He led the NFL with three punt returns for touchdowns, including a league-best 90-yard run to 'the house' against Philadelphia. His yards per punt return average of 12.9 was also tops in the league.

But off the field, Jones carried more than a fair share of baggage. In February 2006, he entered into a physical confrontation with a policeman in Fayetteville, Georgia, outside the home of his pregnant girlfriend. Jones threw a punch at the officer before being handcuffed. He later pleaded no contest to a charge of obstructing a police officer and was given three years' probation plus a $500 fine. An additional charge of marijuana possession was dropped.

Six months later, in the last week of the pre-season, Jones was accused of assault after he allegedly spat on a woman in a Murfreesboro, Tennessee night club. He was arrested for public intoxication and disorderly conduct.

Then, in October, a similar incident occurred at an establishment in Nashville as Jones again faced a misdemeanour assault charge for spitting in a woman's face. As a result of both incidents, Jones received six months' probation plus a one-game suspension from the Titans team.

Although he was only two years into a professional career in the NFL, Jones's rap sheet would only continue to grow.

THE CRIME...

Jones was in Las Vegas during the NBA's All-Star weekend in 2007. On February 19, he visited the Minxx Gentlemen's Club and Lounge and began throwing large wads of cash at more than 40 strippers on the stage. Court documents later showed that Jones's intent was merely to shower the scantily-clad women as a visual effect. But the promoter who hired the strippers began collecting the money and retrieved a huge sum before leaving the premises.

A huge melee broke out after Jones became incensed that he had lost the cash,

Did You Know...?

During an NFL rookie symposium in 2012, Jones was asked to share his experiences with first-year players. As told to *Sports Illustrated*, he credited Goodell with changing him as a person and accepted full responsibility for his actions that got him suspended. He also estimated that 90 percent of his childhood friends were either dead or in jail.

If the $80,000 that Jones used to "make it rain" on strippers in a Las Vegas club was exorbitant, the sum paled in comparison to the $1 million that he admitted to his audience to spending in just one weekend. Jones's co-guest speaker on the symposium panel, former teammate and star receiver Terrell Owens, turned to him and said, "Man, you crazy!"

By 2013, "Pacman" appeared to be making the most out of the opportunities he had been granted to clean up his act, starting in all 16 of Cincinnati's games. However, another blemish on his record – a September citation for disorderly conduct during a traffic stop – indicated that his frequent pattern of off-field issues hasn't totally abated.

which totaled more than $80,000. According to police, Jones threatened four people while inside the club. Two of those threatened were security guards who were trying to break up a scuffle between a woman in Jones's party and one of the strippers. Jones reportedly reached behind his back to simulate that he was carrying a weapon.

The chaotic scene turned even uglier as shots were fired outside the club by an unknown gunman. Three people were injured by the bullets. One of the victims was the club manager, Thomas Urbanski, who was left paralyzed from the waist down.

Following a police investigation, Jones was charged in June on two felony counts of coercion. The scope of the charges was limited to only the events inside the club and not outside where the shooting occurred. Nevertheless, "Pacman" still faced as many as twelve years in prison.

WHAT FOLLOWED...

NFL Commissioner Roger Goodell levied his own sanction against Jones even before the legal charges were formerly filed, suspending "Pacman" for the entire 2007 season.

"We must protect the integrity of the NFL," Goodell said in a statement. "The highest standards of conduct must be met by everyone in the NFL because it is a privilege to represent the NFL, not a right. These players, and all members of our league, have to make the right choices and decisions in their conduct on a consistent basis."

Jones forfeited his salary of just under $1.3 million for the year. At the time of the suspension, he had been the subject of no fewer than ten police investigations for off-field incidents, the Las Vegas shooting merely being the most serious and publicized one.

Jones was reinstated by Goodell for the beginning of the 2008 season. The Titans cut loose their ties with the problematic player, however, trading him to Dallas. But he was suspended again for off-field conduct and eventually checked into an alcohol rehabilitation centre. The Cowboys released him at the end of the year. Jones didn't return to the NFL again until 2010 when he signed in Cincinnati, where he has played ever since.

After arranging a deal to plead guilty to one gross misdemeanour charge of disorderly conduct, Jones was sentenced to one year probation plus 200 hours of community service for his role in the Las Vegas incident.

CHRIS HENRY

6'2"

B. BELLE CHASSE, LOUISIANA, MAY 17, 1983

D. CHARLOTTE, NORTH CAROLINA, DECEMBER 17, 2009

6'0"

COLLEGE: WEST VIRGINIA

5'10"

DRAFTED IN 3RD ROUND,

83RD OVERALL BY

5'8"

CINCINNATI IN 2005

314286R

5'6"

WIDE RECEIVER

5'4"

HT:6'4" WT:197 lbs

IN THE BEGINNING...

Although Chris Henry played just two seasons with West Virginia University, he was one of the most dangerous receivers in the Big East Conference during his time with the Mountaineers. In his freshman year of 2003, Henry's average mark of 24.5 yards per reception led the conference and was third-best in the NCAA. Henry also ranked second in the Big East in receiving yards (1,006) and receiving touchdowns (10).

For an encore the following year, Henry caught 12 touchdowns to lead the conference. He also finished in the top ten in several major offensive categories, including receiving yards (4th), receptions (6th), and yards from scrimmage (10th). With future NFL return man "Pacman" Jones also on the roster, the Mountaineers ended their season with a loss in the Gator Bowl for a second straight year.

Henry was drafted by the Cincinnati Bengals in 2005 but was relegated to being a third-stringer behind veteran wide-outs Chad Johnson and T.J. Houshmandzadeh. Nevertheless, Henry managed to appear in 14 of the team's games – five as a starter – catching six passes for touchdowns and averaging 13.6 yards per catch. The Bengals won the AFC North Division with an 11-5 record, losing their wild card playoff game at home to the Pittsburgh Steelers, the eventual Super Bowl champions.

Away from Paul Brown Stadium, however, Henry became a problem. Late in the regular season he had been arrested for marijuana possession in Covington, Kentucky. He pleaded guilty and was fined $250 while also serving 28 days in a drug rehabilitation program.

Then, on January 29, 2006, Henry was charged with possession of a concealed firearm after an altercation outside a night club in Orlando.

Did You Know...?

Following Henry's death, researchers at West Virginia University diagnosed the former football player with chronic traumatic encephalopathy (CTE). The ailment is a form of degenerative brain damage caused by multiple hits to the head. CTE has been the subject of several medical investigations as the NFL addresses league-wide concerns over concussions and brain injuries.

Over 4,500 former players sued the NFL claiming that the league concealed knowledge of the dangers of concussions. The suit alleged that, as a result, players were often rushed into returning from injuries despite not being medically fit. The book "League of Denial" by Mark Fainaru-Wada and Steve Fainaru chronicled the NFL's ongoing concussion saga.

In August 2013, a $765 million settlement was reached between the NFL and the plaintiffs, a sum that – when divided among the number of players – is a relatively paltry $170,000 each, considering the billions of dollars that the league earns in revenues each year and the significant long-term implications of head trauma.

On January 14, 2014, however, Judge Anita Brody denied the preliminary approval for the settlement, citing lack of available documentation regarding the fairness of the amount of the payout.

His third arrest, which occurred the following June, was for driving under the influence of alcohol. Given his three run-ins with the law in seven months, it would have been incredible to think that Henry would find himself in a police station again within a couple of weeks. But, that's exactly the scenario that occurred just ten days after his DUI booking.

THE CRIME…

On June 14, 2006, Henry was charged with providing alcohol to three underage females. He turned himself in to police after an arrest warrant was issued. The warrant indicated that the girls were aged 18, 16, and 15 and were in his car when he gave them alcohol, knowing that they were all under the legal drinking age of 21. Henry faced three misdemeanour counts of unlawful transaction with a minor.

"You embarrassed a lot of people—teammates, friends and family, the city, the fans, and myself."

His young receiver becoming more troublesome even before his sophomore season, Bengals coach Marvin Lewis voiced his concern. "That bothers me when someone doesn't quite understand social laws," Lewis told the *Associated Press.* "That bothers me, no question."

In a twist to the case, the 18-year-old girl, Monica Beamon, accused Henry of raping her in an incident dating back to April 30. Henry was eventually cleared of the charge after police found inconsistencies in her story, and Beamon was charged with filing a false police report.

In August, Beamon was accused of murder after she allegedly stabbed a man, Louis

Carcelli, over a money dispute during a prostitution transaction. She pleaded guilty and was sentenced to life in prison, with no possibility of parole for at least 15 years.

Henry was able to escape jail time for his previous three arrests, but not for the incident involving Beamon and the other two girls. He received a two-day sentence behind bars and also agreed to give speeches to schoolchildren.

"You embarrassed yourself," Judge Greg Grothaus told Henry. "You embarrassed a lot of people—teammates, friends and family, the city, the fans, and myself."

WHAT FOLLOWED...

Despite missing two games in 2006 due to a suspension handed down by the NFL for violation of the league's substance-abuse policy, Henry caught 36 passes for 605 yards, including nine touchdowns. As the results of his various criminal proceedings were rendered, Henry received an additional eight-game suspension to begin the 2007 campaign as part of a personal-conduct policy mandated by league commissioner Roger Goodell.

When Henry was arrested again in 2008, this time for reportedly assaulting an 18-year-old man, he was released by Cincinnati. "Chris Henry has forfeited his opportunity to pursue a career with the Bengals," team president Mike Brown said in a statement. "His conduct can no longer be tolerated." After the charges were dropped, however, Henry re-signed with the club.

As the 2009 season drew to a close, Henry was sidelined with a forearm injury. On December 16, he was involved in a domestic dispute with his fiancée, Loleini Tonga. Police said he jumped into the back of a pickup truck as Tonga was driving away from their home. About a minute later, Henry was lying unconscious in the road. He died of his injuries the next day. No charges were filed against Tonga in the tragedy.

Coach Lewis mourned the loss of the 26-year-old, once promising receiver. "It's a very difficult thing with his loss and a young life and one that won't ever get to reach its full potential," he said.

FROSTEE RUCKER

6'2"

B. TUSTIN, CALIFORNIA, SEPTEMBER 14, 1983

COLLEGE: UNIVERSITY OF

6'0"

SOUTHERN CALIFORNIA

5'10"

DRAFTED IN 3RD ROUND,

91ST OVERALL BY

5'8"

CINCINNATI IN 2006

270603R

5'6"

DEFENSIVE END

5'4"

HT:6'3"   WT:270 lbs

IN THE BEGINNING...

Frostee Rucker proved his versatility during his senior year at Tustin High School, earning all-star selections as both a running back and linebacker during an MVP season. Upon graduation, he enrolled at Colorado State but ended up transferring to USC. In his sophomore year of 2003, Rucker switched positions, from linebacker to defensive end.

The change was beneficial for the Trojans as Rucker made 29 tackles that season to go along with one interception on the stats sheet. Under coach Pete Carroll, and with quarterback Matt Leinart at the helm, USC won the national championship, defeating Michigan in the Rose Bowl.

The Trojans won a second consecutive title in 2004, going undefeated and crushing Oklahoma, 55-19, in the Orange Bowl. Leinart won the Heisman Trophy as the best college player in the country. By 2005, Rucker was habitually making life miserable for opposing quarterbacks, finishing seventh in the Pac-10 Conference with six sacks, on the way to a First Team All Pac-10 selection. Meanwhile, Rucker's teammate, Reggie Bush, became USC's second consecutive Heisman Trophy winner.

The powerhouse Trojans advanced to the Rose Bowl, bidding for a third consecutive national title. USC battled the University of Texas Longhorns for the national championship in a back-and-forth epic. Late in the fourth quarter, Texas quarterback Vince Young ran into the end zone on a fourth-down play to score the winning touchdown, the Longhorns prevailing 41-38 to end USC's run at the top.

Three months later in April 2006, the Cincinnati Bengals made Rucker a third-round selection at the NFL draft, but Rucker made the wrong headlines before even stepping onto the field for his first professional training camp.

 THE CRIME...

On June 20, 2006, misdemeanour charges were filed against Rucker after an alleged fight took place between him and his then-girlfriend Joelle Barchan. A spokesman from the Los Angeles city attorney's office indicated that Barchan sustained minor injuries. Two mobile devices were also damaged in the altercation.

Rucker faced two counts each of battery and vandalism, while a charge of false imprisonment was also added for good measure. Facing a maximum penalty of three years in jail, he denied all charges.

The trial began the following September, at which time a history of previous allegations against Rucker came to light. His transfer from Colorado State to USC had come as a result of a 2002 accusation against him of sexual assault against a female student. That case was plea bargained to a misdemeanour charge of harassment, and Rucker was given a one-year suspended sentence.

Barchan told the *Columbus Dispatch* that she caught Rucker cheating on her, six months into their relationship. "Then he got aggressive with me," she said. "He actually struck me. I was real mad and stayed away for a while, but he begged and

Did You Know...?

The 2006 Rose Bowl, Rucker's final college game, ranks as one of the greatest games in college football history. USC was vying for a third consecutive national title against Texas, the defending Rose Bowl champions. Both teams had gone undefeated heading into the game, the only two NCAA Division I-A teams to accomplish the feat that year.

This was the first college game in history to feature two Heisman Trophy winners – Matt Leinart (2004) and Reggie Bush (2005) – playing for the same team. USC was clinging to a 38-33 lead in the fourth quarter and Texas driving down the field. Longhorns quarterback Vince Young marched Texas down to the nine-yard line with just 26 seconds remaining. Facing a fourth down and needing five yards, Young scampered into the right corner of the end zone for the game-winning touchdown in one of the most memorable plays of all-time.

Adding insult to injury for USC, the school was asked to disassociate itself from Bush after it was discovered that the running back had received gifts from an agent during his college career. In June 2010 the NCAA levied sanctions against the institution that resulted in the eventual forfeiture of Bush's Heisman Trophy. All 12 of the wins that were earned during the Trojans' 2005 season that ended with the Rose Bowl loss to Texas were wiped from the record books. USC was also banned from bowl games for a two-year period and lost 30 football scholarships over three years.

Two months after the sanctions were announced, USC removed Bush's jersey from Los Angeles Memorial Coliseum. Bush had vowed to return a replica copy of the Heisman Trophy that he had been given upon first receiving the award, but he held onto it until August 2012.

begged and begged for me to come back, and I went back."

After a repeated cycle of violence, Barchan left Rucker and returned to her hometown of Miami in the fall of the next year. But Rucker then sought a restraining order against Barchan, saying that she had sent him numerous threatening e-mails and made several phone calls to him. The order was never filed because Barchan had already moved.

WHAT FOLLOWED...

Rucker accepted a bargain on April 30, 2007, to plead no contest to one count of vandalism plus the false imprisonment charge, while the other charges were dropped. He was sentenced to three years' probation and 750 hours of community service and fined $250. Rucker was also ordered to get treatment for domestic violence issues.

The NFL initially suspended Rucker for Cincinnati's season opener that year against the Baltimore Ravens, but the suspension was overturned upon an appeal. Peter Schaffer, who represented Rucker in his case to counsel designated by Commissioner Roger Goodell, successfully argued that the NFL's personal-conduct policy did not apply to actions that occurred prior to a player's entry into the league. Rucker also had the support of Bengals head coach Marvin Lewis, who testified on his behalf.

"We presented a comprehensive case with many different factors, and at the end of the day the hearing officer agreed with us and rescinded the suspension," said Schaffer.

The case was just one of many black eyes for the image of the Bengals franchise. As many as ten players had faced criminal charges during a 14-month stretch between January 2006 and March 2007.

Rucker accepted a bargain on April 30, 2007, to plead no contest to one count of vandalism plus the false imprisonment charge, while the other charges were dropped.

KOREN ROBINSON

6'2"

B. BELMONT, CALIFORNIA, MARCH 19, 1980

6'0"

COLLEGE: NORTH CAROLINA

STATE

5'10"

DRAFTED IN 1ST ROUND,

9TH OVERALL BY SEATTLE

5'8"

IN 2001

679232R

5'6"

WIDE RECEIVER

5'4"

HT:6'1"   WT:205 lbs

VIKINGS

IN THE BEGINNING...

In his 1999 freshman year with the North Carolina State Wolfpack, Koren Robinson was asked to make a transition from tailback – where he had played all through high school – to wide receiver. Under the mentorship of outgoing graduate Torry Holt, who had been selected by the Detroit Lions in the NFL draft that year, Robinson adjusted to the new role with startling ease, finishing in the top 10 in the Atlantic Coast Conference in receptions (6th, with 48) and receiving yards (5th, with 753).

His second year was even more productive, Robinson's 13 receiving touchdowns as the fifth-best total in the NCAA. The Wolfpack had an 8-4 record, defeating Minnesota 38-30 in the PC Micron Bowl.

Following his outstanding sophomore season, Robinson made the bold move of declaring himself eligible for the 2001 NFL draft, aspiring to be the first overall pick. While that distinction eventually went to quarterback Michael Vick from

Virginia Tech, the Seattle Seahawks scooped up Robinson eight spots later. Seattle didn't hedge its bets on the investment, signing Robinson to a six-year, $10.1 million contract.

Robinson earned a spot on the Seahawks' roster as the number two receiver behind Darrell Jackson, catching 39 passes for 536 yards. His second NFL season, 2002, appeared to be a breakthrough year as he racked up 1,240 yards in the air. Robinson's average of 15.9 yards per catch was tenth-best in the league.

However, away from the gridiron, Robinson had run-ins with the law and habitually missed team meetings. His production was well short of what Seattle fans had seen during Robinson`s sophomore year. In 2004, Robinson was suspended for four games by the NFL for violating the league's substance-abuse policy.

"It's very disappointing to see wonderful potential lost like that," Seahawks coach Mike Holmgren told KOMO news in Seattle. "Is he going to rebound off this? Yes, but this is a missed time. You just want the lights to go on for some of these young guys and have them understand how fortunate they are to be doing what they're doing."

Did You Know...?

Robinson briefly resumed his career in the United Football League, playing for the Florida Tuskers. One of his teammates in the upstart league was Tatum Bell, who played running back for both Denver and Detroit in the NFL and had his own share of off-field issues. The Tuskers traded Robinson to the New York Sentinels. Repeating some of his behaviour from his days with the Seahawks, Robinson was suspended by the Sentinels for failing to show up for team meetings.

Upon retirement, Robinson's troubles, in addition to his alcohol abuse, were compounded by financial matters. In June 2010, the *Charlotte Observer* reported that Robinson owed nearly $500,000 in taxes to the state of North Carolina, where he had enjoyed his college success.

Robinson was reported as the state's third-worst tax delinquent on a list of offenders who collectively owed the state more than $841 million.

The last straw for the Seahawks was an arrest of Robinson in 2005 for drunk driving, which led to his release from the team. He was signed by Minnesota and was inserted into the lineup as a kick returner to complement his wide receiver duties. Robinson responded by having a Pro Bowl season that included a pair of kick returns for touchdowns. The change of scenery appeared to be beneficial for the former Seahawk.

THE CRIME...

The Vikings had signed Robinson to a three-year, $12.7 million deal, convinced that the player's off-field issues were behind him. But on August 15, 2006, Robinson was arrested after police clocked his BMW going 104 miles per hour in a 55 mph zone. He was charged with a felony count of fleeing from police, two charges for driving while under the influence , and three other misdemeanours.

"When he was with us, I rooted for him. I tried to help him. I felt I kind of failed the kid somehow."

According to police reports obtained by the *Associated Press*, two officers in St. Peter, Minnesota gave chase after Robinson's blue BMW sedan was traveling so quickly that its speed could not be detected by radar. The pursuit continued along Highway 169 as the BMW eluded police beyond a curve in the road.

A few miles south, in Mankato – the site of the Vikings' training facility – the BMW ran a red light. Finally an officer, who was waiting for Robinson's vehicle, pulled the car over after setting up an advance post at a road leading to the training camp. Robinson was arrested at gunpoint, without resistance. His blood-alcohol level measured 0.11 percent.

Robinson had been speeding to meet the team's 11:00pm curfew. The initial police radar reading occurred at about 10:45. Vikings head coach Brad Childress expressed his frustration. "I couldn't be more disappointed for him, for this football team, and for the community to have that happen," Childress said.

Mike Holmgren, Robinson's former coach in Seattle, was also saddened. "When he was with us, I rooted for him. I tried to help him. I felt I kind of failed the kid somehow," Holmgren said of Robinson. "He's got to get a grip on this before something bad happens."

WHAT FOLLOWED...

Robinson was given a 90-day jail sentence for violating probation. The ruling came as a result of his earlier 2005 drunk driving arrest after which he was given five years' probation with the stipulation that he did not consume alcohol or have any other violations.

Minnesota cut Robinson after the incident, and he was signed by NFC North Division rival Green Bay in the second week of the 2006 season. But after playing in four games for the Packers, the league handed down a one-year suspension without pay for violating the NFL's substance-abuse policy.

Robinson returned to the Green Bay to play nine games in 2007. The next year, he finished his NFL career with the team that drafted him, Seattle, with a 12-game stint, catching for 400 yards and two touchdowns.

STEVE FOLEY

6'2"

B. Little Rock, Arkansas, September 11, 1975

College: Northeast Louisiana

6'0"

(now Louisiana-Monroe)

5'10"

Drafted in 3rd round,

75th overall by

5'8"

Cincinnati in 1998

511286F

5'6"

LINEBACKER

5'4"

HT:6'4" WT:265 lbs

IN THE BEGINNING...

Steve Foley had an outstanding senior year in college playing for the Northeast Louisiana Warhawks, recording 18.5 sacks to lead the NCAA. Five-and-a-half of those sacks came in one game, establishing a school record. Although Foley was on the Cincinnati Bengals' roster in 1998, the year the team drafted him, he started just one game in his rookie season.

The linebacker became a full-time player in 1999, making 34 tackles and registering three-and-a-half sacks. The progress was good news for Foley on an individual level, but the team was awful. Cincinnati finished the year with a 4-12 record while the defence gave up 460 points, or 28.8 per game, the most allowed by any club in the 31-team NFL.

More significantly, Foley had his share of legal troubles. In April 1999, he was arrested for failing to appear in court for a child support case. He was released on bond but was arrested the next morning for driving while under the influence. A third arrest came just ten months later when Foley was charged with domestic violence.

Police alleged that Foley kicked open a door where his son lived with the child's mother, although the player denied the charges. Two months later, he was accused of firing a handgun in the air outside a night club and was charged with a misdemeanour count of disturbing the peace by drunk and disorderly conduct. This marked his fourth booking in a calendar year.

After four years with the Bengals, Foley signed with Houston, playing with the Texans for one season before joining the San Diego Chargers in 2004. As he did with the Warhawks in Louisiana, Foley terrorized opposing quarterbacks. His ten sacks led the Chargers team, and the total was second in the NFL among linebackers. San Diego rewarded him with a three-year contract extension worth $10 million.

The 2005 Chargers finished with a respectable 9-7 record but out of the play-offs. As the 2006 campaign was about to get underway, Foley's career and life were both irreparably damaged.

 THE CRIME...

On September 3, 2006, Foley was followed by 23-year-old rookie police officer Aaron Mansker from downtown San Diego to Foley's home in nearby Poway. Mansker was driving his personal Mazda and wearing a T-shirt and jeans. The officer twice drove up next to Foley's Oldsmobile, ordering the player to pull over, but both times the officer was rebuffed. The two men engaged in a confrontation just outside of Foley's residence. Foley was shot in his leg, hip, and hand.

Foley's companion in the car, Lisa Gault, was arrested on suspicion of assault with a deadly weapon and driving under the influence after accusations that she attempted to run over Mansker with the Oldsmobile.

The day after the shooting, the Chargers placed Foley on non-football injured reserve. San Diego general manager A.J. Smith said that his player wouldn't be

Did You Know...?

Foley's legal troubles continued in 2008 after two of his pit bulls attacked a woman and killed her puppy. Twana Schulz sustained bite marks to her face and neck. She tried to hold on to her dog, but the pit bulls jerked it from her hands. "I had to decide on whether it was my life or the dog's, and I had to let my puppy go," Schulz told the *Houston Chronicle*.

Foley was indicted on a charge of "attack by a dog," which was a third-degree felony under "Lillian's Law," a piece of Texas legislation that was passed in 2007 which provided harsh penalties of up to 20 years in prison for owners negligently allowing their dogs to cause harm or death to others. The law was instituted following a horrifying incident in which a 76-year-old grandmother, Lillian Stiles, was attacked and killed by dogs on her own front yard.

The charges against Foley were dropped after an out-of-court settlement with Schulz was reached.

paid because the injuries that were sustained weren't related to football. Foley was due his base salary of $775,000 plus a roster bonus of $875,000.

"Obviously this is a big blow," Smith told the *Associated Press*. "It's a tragedy in itself, as far as the player is concerned. And it's a blow to our football team."

Foley was charged with misdemeanour drunk driving after blood-alcohol tests determined that he had a reading of 0.23 percent, nearly three times the legal limit in California of 0.08 percent.

WHAT FOLLOWED...

Mansker pleaded guilty to the drunk driving charge and was given five years' probation. Lisa Gault was convicted of assault with a deadly weapon and was sentenced to six months in jail and five years' probation.

The shooting injuries ended Foley's playing career. In 2007, Foley sued Mansker and his employer, the City of Coronado. The suit sought millions of dollars in general and special damages, including medical expenses, as well as the "loss of both past and future earnings." Meanwhile, the Chargers terminated Foley's contract.

At both the criminal trial and civil trials, Foley's attorney and Mansker gave conflicting testimony. Foley's lawyer, Harvey Levine, contended that his client did not abide by Mansker's instructions because the latter did not identify himself as a police officer. Mansker countered by saying that he identified himself accordingly but did not flash his badge.

Mansker testified that he shot Foley when the player reached towards his waistband. Foley was not carrying any weapon. The district attorney of San Diego County did not pursue criminal charges against Mansker, saying that the shooting was in self-defence.

Foley's lawyer, Harvey Levine, contended that his client did not abide by Mansker's instructions because the latter did not identify himself as a police officer.

Just as Foley was scheduled to testify on his own behalf, a settlement in the case was reached for $5.5 million. He moved to Houston to care for his 11-year-old daughter and work towards finishing his college degree.

Mansker returned to the Coronado police force. Foley's lawyers had contended that the rookie officer, who had been off-duty at the time of the shooting, violated his training procedure by attempting to pull Foley over instead of just following him. A further review by Coronado resulted in the stipulation that off-duty officers in similar situations must wait for uniformed police personnel to arrive in a marked vehicle before making a stop on a suspect.

JARED ALLEN

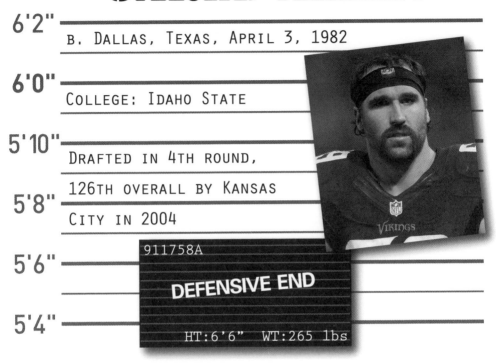

6'2"
B. DALLAS, TEXAS, APRIL 3, 1982

6'0"
COLLEGE: IDAHO STATE

5'10"
DRAFTED IN 4TH ROUND,

126TH OVERALL BY KANSAS
5'8"
CITY IN 2004

911758A

5'6"
DEFENSIVE END

5'4"
HT:6'6" WT:265 lbs

IN THE BEGINNING...

As a college player, Jared Allen was a two-time All-American with the Idaho State Bengals. A stalwart on the defensive line, he led the NCAA in sacks and forced fumbles during his senior year of 2003. He graduated as the school's career sack leader and was drafted by the Kansas City Chiefs the following April.

NFL quarterbacks quickly became accustomed to Allen's ferocity and bulking 6'6" frame. He racked up nine sacks in his rookie season in 2004 and then followed with a superb sophomore year in which he registered eleven sacks, the ninth-best total in the league.

The 2006 campaign showed that Allen could not only bring down ball carriers – making 66 tackles in all – but also that he was quick to pounce on a loose pigskin. His total of six fumble recoveries was best in the NFL. Nevertheless, heading into the final week of the season, the Chiefs' playoff hopes looked grim.

With a logjam in the race for the final wild card berth, Kansas City needed to beat Jacksonville, and get help from three other teams, to qualify. But the teams that they were chasing – Tennessee, Pittsburgh, and heavily-favoured Denver (versus San Francisco) – all lost, sending the Chiefs into the post-season.

The joy of the miracle was erased in Kansas City's 23-8 loss to Indianapolis, the eventual Super Bowl champions. While Allen had a terrific showing on the field, he ran afoul of the law during the team's bye week, prior to the Chiefs' Week 4 game against San Francisco.

THE CRIME...

Allen was charged with driving under the influence following an incident in Leawood, Kansas, on September 26, 2006. The *Kansas City Star* reported that police stopped him at around 1:30am after his Dodge Charger was seen weaving back and forth across the highway, possibly crossing the centre line. Allen refused to take a sobriety or breathalyzer test, resulting in an automatic suspension of his license.

The incident occurred after a night of drinking during which Allen consoled himself following the breakup of a long-term relationship with his girlfriend. It was the second DUI booking for Allen in five months.

On May 11, 2006, Allen faced a similar charge after he was speeding in Overland, Kansas. The charge was dismissed after Allen agreed to refrain from drinking alcohol and not breaking any more laws.

WHAT FOLLOWED...

In February 2007, Allen pleaded no contest to the charges and was sentenced to two days in jail. The NFL suspended him for four games, but an appeal reduced the ban to just two games.

The sequence of events was an eye-opener for Allen, who vowed to change his dangerous habits. As reported by *Sports Illustrated*, Allen underwent counseling at the orders of the league. "It was good self-discovery," Allen said. "Alcohol was obviously a problem because I was always getting in trouble with it. So I figured, let's cut it out." Allen also drastically revised his diet and training, engaging in mixed martial arts as part of his new regimen.

The changes paid huge dividends. Despite missing the first two games of the 2007 season because of the suspension, Allen incredibly led the league with 15.5 sacks. He was also named to the Pro Bowl for the first time in his career.

His four-year tenure in Kansas City ended shortly afterwards. Prior to the arrests, the Chiefs had long-term plans for their defensive standout. But the DUI's changed all of that, and Allen was offered only a one-year term as a restricted free agent.

"Alcohol was obviously a problem because I was always getting in trouble with it. So I figured, let's cut it out."

In 2008, Allen was traded to the Minnesota Vikings for several draft picks, one of which was a first-rounder. Wearing the famed purple jersey of the Vikings, Allen continued to establish himself as one of the most feared pass rushers in the game. He made the Pro Bowl in four of the five seasons between 2008 and 2012. His 2011 season total of 22 sacks was tied for the second-best mark of all time with Mark Gastineau (New York Jets, 1984), just a half-sack behind the record set by Michael Strahan (New York Giants, 2001).

Allen reflected on his turnaround in a 2008 interview with the *San Jose Mercury News*. "After the last DUI, I had to take a long look in the mirror," Allen

Did You Know…?

The trade that sent Allen from Kansas City to Minnesota along with a sixth-round draft pick (John Sullivan, centre) netted the Chiefs a first-round pick (Branden Albert, tackle), two third-rounders (Jamaal Charles, running back, and DaJuan Morgan, safety) and a sixth-rounder (Kevin Robinson, wide receiver).

Albert has been a steady force on the Chiefs' defensive line after an injury-riddled start to his career, making the Pro Bowl in 2013, his fifth pro season.

But the gem in the deal for Kansas City was Charles. A gifted, explosive running back, he evolved into the cornerstone of the Chiefs' offense, earning Pro Bowl nods in three of four seasons from 2010-2013. Over the first six years of his career, Charles had four seasons of rushing for 1,000 yards or more.

Additionally, his 12 touchdowns on the ground and combined total of 19 running and receiving touchdowns led the NFL in 2013. That season, Charles finished third in voting for the offensive player of the year as voted by the *Associated Press*. Peyton Manning, quarterback of the AFC West rival Denver Broncos, won in a landslide.

said. "I realized I was throwing away everything I love, and for what? I had always been afraid to grow up and have a normal life. But I realized it was finally time."

It was Ray Allen, the player's grandfather, who sternly reprimanded Jared following the second arrest, shaming him into getting sober. "You're screwing up this family's name. Now what are you going to do about it?" Ray asked his grandson. "If you want to be the best, then start acting like the best. It's time to be a football player only. You can't be the town drunk."

By the end of the 2013 season, Allen's 128.5 career sacks ranked him 12th on the NFL's all-time list, second among active players to John Abraham's 133.5. Allen was also tied with two other players – Ted Hendricks and Doug English – for most career safeties (four each). In March 2014, Allen signed with the Chicago Bears as a free agent.

JERRAMY STEVENS

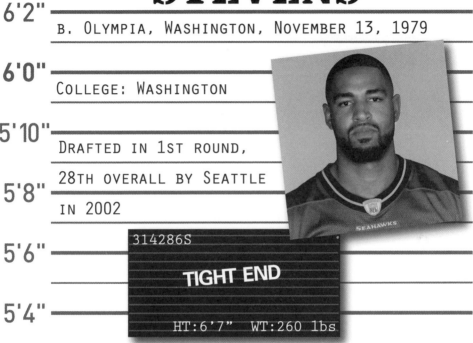

6'2" — B. OLYMPIA, WASHINGTON, NOVEMBER 13, 1979

6'0" — COLLEGE: WASHINGTON

5'10" — DRAFTED IN 1ST ROUND,

5'8" — 28TH OVERALL BY SEATTLE
IN 2002

314286S

5'6" —

TIGHT END

5'4" —

HT:6'7" WT:260 lbs

IN THE BEGINNING...

Jerramy Stevens enjoyed a collegiate career playing for the University of Washington Huskies, becoming one of the best tight ends in the school's history. In 2000, he caught 43 passes for 600 yards and scored three touchdowns on the way to a semi-finalist nomination for the inaugural John Mackey Award presented to the best tight end in college football. The nod eventually went to Tim Stratton of Purdue.

The Seattle Seahawks chose Stevens in the first round of the 2002 draft, despite the player having a history of legal issues. As a high school student, Stevens was charged with felony assault after stomping on a boy's head as the victim lay unconscious. The case was pleaded down to a misdemeanour. While a student at UW, Stevens served five days of a 90-day jail sentence after leaving the scene of an accident in which he crashed his car into a nursing home.

The most serious accusation against him, even before Stevens turned professional, came in July 2000 when he was arrested on charges of sexual assault. The *Seattle Times* reported that several witnesses saw Stevens having sex with a university freshman, identified only by her middle name, Marie.

The female student looked "drugged or drunk, half passed out, eyes glazed," which was symptomatic of being under the influence of a date rape drug. But prosecutors couldn't find any conclusive evidence to press charges, primarily because blood tests on the alleged victim were conducted too late. Four years later, Stevens settled a civil suit filed by his accuser for $300,000.

Stevens played five seasons in Seattle, catching 15 touchdowns in 71 games while wearing a Seahawks uniform. In Super Bowl XL, he caught three passes, including one for a 16-yard touchdown, but he also dropped three passes as Seattle fell, 21-10, to the Pittsburgh Steelers.

Did You Know...?

Stevens's wife Hope Solo won a gold medal playing on the U.S. Olympic soccer team that competed in Beijing in 2008, and repeated the feat in London in 2012. But the latter achievement came amidst some controversy in the semi-finals in which the United States was matched against Canada.

The underdog Canadians led 3-2 heading into the 78th minute on the strength of a game for the ages by Christine Sinclair, who had scored all three goals for Canada. But Norwegian referee Christina Pedersen inexplicably called Canadian goalkeeper Erin McLeod for a six-second violation for delay of game. The call led to a free kick for the U.S., resulting in a handball which led to a penalty kick awarded to American Megan Rapinoe.

Rapinoe promptly tied the game, forcing extra time. When it appeared that the match was moving towards a penalty kick shootout, American striker Alex Morgan headed the ball into the net past McLeod in the 123rd minute, breaking the hearts of Canadians and sending the Americans to the gold-medal game.

Even U.S. coach Pia Sundhage was incredulous at the six-second violation call that turned the game's momentum. "I have never seen that before," she said.

Canada defeated France in the bronze-medal game after Diana Matheson scored the match's only goal to salvage a place on the podium for her country.

THE CRIME...

Fourteen months after playing in the Super Bowl, Stevens's reckless behaviour behind the wheel caught up with him once again. On March 13, 2007, he was arrested in Scottsdale, Arizona on suspicion of drunk driving. Police stopped his car after they noticed the vehicle moving erratically. He refused a breathalyzer test until a warrant was obtained, at which point Stevens measured a level of 0.20, two-and-a-half times Arizona's legal limit.

Stevens faced a minimum sentence of 30 days in jail because the case came under the state's "extreme" intoxication rule which provided for harsher penalties for blood-alcohol levels of 0.15 or higher. The Seahawks released Stevens shortly after the incident.

"I thought the young man had a lot of ability," Seattle coach Mike Holmgren told the *Associated Press*. "And, at the risk of shocking everybody, I thought he was making great strides on and off the field. But at the same time, he is his own worst enemy."

During the 2007 off-season, Stevens signed with the Tampa Bay Buccaneers as a free agent.

WHAT FOLLOWED...

In September 2007, Stevens was found guilty of the three DUI charges levied against him. He was sentenced to 12 days in jail – less than half the minimum time that he had been facing – and was fined $3,160. The sentence reduction was contingent on Stevens completing a rehabilitation program.

Stevens played three full seasons with Tampa Bay as well as the first five games of the 2010 campaign. His last NFL game was in Week 5 when the Buccaneers were pounded by New Orleans, 31-6. On the eve of the Bucs next game versus St. Louis, Stevens was arrested yet again, this time on charges of marijuana possession and possession with intent to sell. Both charges were felonies, while a charge of possession of drug paraphernalia was also filed.

In November 2012, Stevens was arrested on charges of assault against his fiancée, Hope Solo, an Olympic gold medalist with the United States soccer team.

The Buccaneers wasted no time in cutting Stevens from their roster. "It's always tough to see anybody on your team leave for whatever reason," said head coach Raheem Morris, "but you always have to go out and do what's best for the Tampa Bay Buccaneers."

Stevens never returned to the NFL. He was given probation ending in October 2013 as a result of the drug charges.

In November 2012, Stevens was arrested on charges of assault against his fiancée, Hope Solo, an Olympic gold medalist with the United States soccer team. Officers in Kirkland, Washington responded to a 911 call involving several people at a house party. Police found Solo with a lacerated elbow and arrested Stevens based on information provided by witnesses.

However, a judge dismissed the assault charge the next day based on insufficient evidence. The day after the incident, Stevens and Solo were married. Stevens was arrested once more towards the end of that month as a result of the incident violating his previous probation, but no further charges were filed.

Throughout the ordeal, Solo stood by her husband. "I feel bad for all the ignorance in the world," she said. "People are so quick to judge. The media spins stories in such dramatic fashion. I will continue to show love and never make judgments."

FRED EVANS

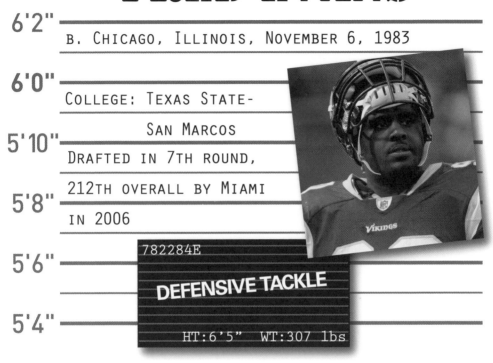

6'2"

B. CHICAGO, ILLINOIS, NOVEMBER 6, 1983

6'0"

COLLEGE: TEXAS STATE-
SAN MARCOS

5'10"

DRAFTED IN 7TH ROUND,
212TH OVERALL BY MIAMI

5'8"

IN 2006

5'6"

782284E

DEFENSIVE TACKLE

5'4"

HT:6'5" WT:307 lbs

IN THE BEGINNING...

Fred Evans split his college time between College of DuPage and Texas State-San Marcos, transferring to the latter school in 2004. In ten games, he registered 17.5 tackles for loss, the fifth-highest total in the NCAA Division I-AA that season. The following season, his senior year, Evans was named an All-American and also named to the Southland Conference First Team for a second consecutive year.

Evans was a late-round draft pick of the Miami Dolphins in 2006, signing a four-year, $1.67 million contract on July 26. It wasn't until the team's final game of the regular season, on New Year's Eve, that Evans, coming off the bench, made his professional debut. He made a pair of tackles, both against Indianapolis running back Joseph Addai in the Dolphins' 27-22 loss to the Colts.

Miami management believed Evans to be a promising young player and planned to insert him into the defensive rotation for his sophomore year, sharing defensive tackle duties with teammate Keith Traylor. His career with the team, however, was very short-lived.

THE CRIME...

Evans was arrested on June 23, 2007, after he had an alleged argument with a cab driver. He was facing four charges: trespassing, disorderly conduct, resisting arrest

Did You Know...?

Evans comes from a bloodline that has the good fortune of being blessed with gifted athletic talent. His sister Aja is an Olympic bobsledder, the breakman in the two-man event. At the 2014 Winter Olympics in Sochi, Russia, Aja Evans and Jamie Greubel won the bronze medal, sliding down the track in the USA-2 sled. Canadians Kallie Humphries and Heather Moyse took their second consecutive gold medal in the event, while Elana Myers and Lauryn Williams in USA-1 won silver.

Fred and Aja Evans' father – Frederick H. Evans – was the first National Association of Intercollegiate Athletics national champion in swimming. He also has the distinction of being the first African-American national collegiate champion. The senior Evans was a three-time NCAA Division II national champion, starring at Chicago State University from 1974-1978. He was inducted into the International Swimming Hall of Fame in 1983.

The siblings' uncle is Gary Matthews, who played 16 Major League Baseball seasons for five different teams: San Francisco, Atlanta, Philadelphia, Chicago (Cubs), and Seattle. Matthews – nicknamed "Sarge" – won the 1973 National League rookie of the year award and was the 1983 National League Championship Series MVP for Philadelphia when the Phillies beat the Los Angeles Dodgers in a four-game series.

Matthews ranked 240th on the all-time list with 234 home runs as of the end of the 2013 season and is enshrined in the Baseball Hall of Fame in Cooperstown, New York. His son Gary Matthews, Jr. – the siblings' cousin – played a dozen years in the major leagues from 1999-2010, collecting 1,056 career hits along the way.

with violence, and battery on a police officer. Miami Beach police were called to the scene following reports of a heated argument between the two individuals. Evans did not leave the cab when police arrived, according to the police report.

Police had to use tasers to subdue Evans after he resisted the initial arrest. The player engaged in a physical confrontation with the officers who tried to place handcuffs on him, biting one policeman on the wrist. At least two officers received bruises during the struggle.

Miami head coach Cam Cameron vented his anger in a prepared release. "We will not condone this type of behaviour. I assure everyone it will be dealt with seriously," he said. Making matters worse, it was revealed just days later that Evans was on probation for a marijuana possession charge stemming from a February arrest in Colorado County, Texas. Evans had pleaded no contest to a count of misdemeanour possession.

Five days after the tasering arrest, Evans was released by the club.

WHAT FOLLOWED...

Evans signed with the Minnesota Vikings as a free agent in August 2007. Following the team's game in Week 12, Evans received a two-game suspension for violating the NFL's personal-conduct policy, stemming from his off-season arrests. He made a total of eleven appearances that year but did not start in any of the games because the Vikings already employed a pair of Pro Bowl tackles in the form of Pat Williams and Kevin Williams.

In 2008, Evans played in all 16 games for the first time in his career and was twice inserted into the lineup as a starter. The Vikings finished with a 10-6 record and made the playoffs for the first time in four years, losing a wild card game to Philadelphia.

The next year, Evans was used solely as a bench player as the Vikings won twelve games to earn the second seed in the NFC. Minnesota destroyed Dallas,

34-3, in the wild card game, earning a berth in the conference championship.

The game featured a matchup of Pro Bowl quarterbacks in the Vikings' Brett Favre and his counterpart Drew Brees of the top-seeded New Orleans Saints. The two pivots combined for 507 passing yards in a contest that was decided by the foot of Saints kicker Garrett Hartley in overtime, New Orleans prevailing, 31-28. Two weeks, later the Saints defeated the Colts in Super Bowl XLIV.

Evans remained on the Minnesota roster through to the end of the 2013 season, even though he earned only an occasional start. The three appearances that he made in 2013 were a career high. Meanwhile, the Vikings franchise has made just once playoff appearance since losing to Brees in the classic NFC showdown, a wild card loss to Green Bay at the end of 2012.

Evans remained on the Minnesota roster through to the end of the 2013 season, even though he earned only an occasional start.

In December 2013, Evans and a cab driver made headlines once again, but for completely different reasons than the incident six years earlier. The *Minneapolis Star Tribune* reported that Evans was getting "frisky" with a woman in a cab driven by Abdikadir Noor. The two passengers had been picked up from Augie's strip club in downtown Minneapolis.

Noor dropped off his clients at their hotel in Eden Prairie, expecting them to return shortly to pay the fare. The pair never returned. Noor first contacted police, then called the Vikings' offices directly hoping for a more efficient resolution. He received his due fare from the club – including a generous tip – totaling about $275.

MICHAEL VICK

6'2"

B. NEWPORT NEWS, VIRGINIA, JUNE 26, 1980

6'0"

COLLEGE: VIRGINIA TECH

5'10"

DRAFTED 1ST OVERALL

BY ATLANTA IN 2001

5'8"

660382V

QUARTERBACK

5'6"

5'4"

HT:6'   WT:215 lbs

IN THE BEGINNING...

Michael Vick was one of four children in a family that grew up in a depressed city in Virginia plagued by crime. His love of football began early, though, and he saw sports as a way to avoid the dangers of Newport News. Vick was the starting quarterback at Warwick High School for three years and rose to prominence as a prospect of great promise. He received impressive scholarship offers from both Syracuse University and Virginia Tech, opting for the latter because of a greater opportunity to develop as a redshirt (i.e., less pressure than what might have been expected of him at Syracuse).

Vick played two seasons as the starting QB for Virginia Tech, in 1999 and 2000, and was so impressive that he solidified his place as the top college player in the U.S. The Atlanta Falcons selected him first overall at the 2001 draft, the first time in NFL history that the top pick had been used for an African-American quarterback.

During his six seasons in Atlanta, Vick was nothing if not impressive. He had a strong arm and had a sensational completions-to-interceptions ratio, and he was also a first-class runner with the ball. Indeed, in 2006, he became the first quarterback to rush for more than 1,000 yards in a season. The Falcons made the playoffs only twice, however, in 2002 and 2004, winning in the first round before being eliminated each season.

THE CRIME...

Despite being one of the most talented players in the NFL, Vick had his world crash in around him starting on April 25, 2007. On that date, state officials in Virginia discovered evidence that an illegal dog-fighting operation had been active

Did You Know...?

As a member of the Falcons, Vick wrote his way into football folklore by becoming the first ever opposing quarterback of the storied Green Bay Packers to win a playoff game at Lambeau Field. Dating to 1939, Green Bay had won each of their first 13 post-season matches played on their home turf—often informally referred to as the 'tundra.' Heading into the 2002 NFC wild card game, Atlanta was the clear underdog against Green Bay which was led by future Hall of Fame quarter-back Brett Favre. It was 22-year-old Vick's first career playoff appearance, and the chilly, inhospitable conditions at Lambeau Field historically favoured the home team. But Vick silenced the 65,358 'cheeseheads' in attendance by marching the Falcons down the field for an opening-drive touchdown. It was the first time all season that Atlanta had scored on its first possession. The score set the tone for the rest of the game as the visitors dominated. Vick put his stamp on the result by eluding a pass rush from Packers' star defensive end Kabeer Gbaja-Biamila and using his speed to turn what looked like a third down loss into an 11-yard rush for a first down. The game ended in a 27-7 romp for Atlanta. As *Sports Illustrated* reported, Favre said to Vick after the game. "I'm proud of you. You're going to be a superstar in this league."

at a property owned by Vick. The investigation quickly became more serious as it was discovered that abuse, torture, and the killing of dogs had been part of the operation. Vick and others were indicted on charges of violating federal laws which prohibited dog-fighting. The illegal business was called Bad Newz Kennels by Vick and his associates.

On August 24, Vick pleaded guilty to "conspiracy to travel in interstate commerce in aid of unlawful activities, and to sponsor a dog in an animal fighting venture." He further admitted to financing most of the venture, sharing in the profits, and knowledge of the destruction of several dogs that performed poorly.

While free on bail, Vick then tested positive for marijuana in a random test and was confined to his home at nights. On December 10, 2007, Vick was sentenced to 23 months in prison and sent to Leavenworth to serve his time. He was released on July 20, 2009.

Even while in prison Vick was forced into bankruptcy, but upon his release he promised to be a different person.

WHAT FOLLOWED...

Even while in prison Vick was forced into bankruptcy, but upon his release he promised to be a different person. The Falcons had tried unsuccessfully to trade his rights, so in June 2009 he was given his outright release. As a result, after leaving jail he was, in NFL terms, a free agent. A month later, he signed a one-year contract with the Philadelphia Eagles for $1.6 million and was re-instated by the league for the third week of the regular season. Vick, however, was behind starter Donovan

McNabb and played little during the year.

In 2010, Vick's gridiron luck changed. McNabb was traded and number-two QB Kevin Kolb was injured early in the year. Vick took advantage of the opportunity to play and was stellar the rest of the season. One of his most memorable games came in Week 15 of the regular season against the team's fierce division rivals, the New York Giants. Trailing 31-10 in the fourth quarter, the Eagles rallied with three touchdowns to tie the game with just over one minute remaining. Vick threw two touchdown passes while running into the end zone for the other major score. The game ended on a punt return for a touchdown by Philadelphia's DeSean Jackson on the final play of the game.

Vick was named the Eagles' starter for 2011 and signed a six-year, $100 million contract, although a concussion in 2012 and a hamstring injury in 2013 forced him to the sidelines all too often. In March 2014, Vick signed as a free agent with the New York Jets.

JEREMY BRIDGES

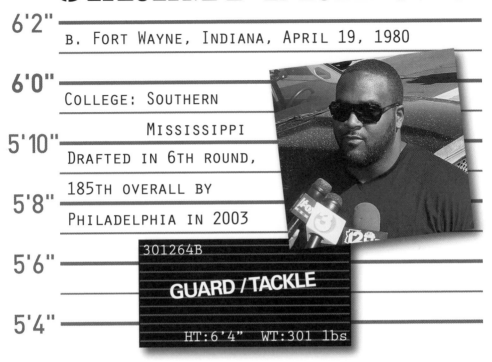

6'2"
B. FORT WAYNE, INDIANA, APRIL 19, 1980

6'0"
COLLEGE: SOUTHERN

MISSISSIPPI

5'10"
DRAFTED IN 6TH ROUND,

185TH OVERALL BY

5'8"
PHILADELPHIA IN 2003

301264B

5'6"
GUARD / TACKLE

5'4"
HT:6'4"   WT:301 lbs

IN THE BEGINNING…

Jeremy Bridges excelled on the gridiron at South Pike High School in Magnolia, Mississippi. In his senior year, 1998, he was named the Pike County player of the year. After graduation, Bridges took his talent on the offensive line to Southern Mississippi where he enjoyed a four-year college career playing for the Golden Eagles. He was redshirted in his freshman year but then started 45 consecutive games between 1999 and 2002.

During that stretch, Southern Mississippi advanced to three bowl games. It won the 1999 Liberty Bowl and 2000 Mobile Alabama Bowl – beating Colorado State and Texas Christian, respectively – while losing to Oklahoma State in the 2002 Houston Bowl. Bridges graduated with a degree in sports administration.

Bridges never played a game for the Philadelphia Eagles, who selected him in the sixth round of the 2003 draft. He was inactive for the entire 2003 season and was claimed off waivers by Arizona on September 6, 2004. In two seasons with the Cardinals, Bridges made 21 appearances, starting in eleven games. He was cut by Arizona prior to the start of the 2006 season, signing with Carolina when the Panthers' starting left tackle, Travelle Wharton, was lost for the year after suffering a devastating knee injury in the team's season opener.

Carolina finished out of the playoffs with a record of 8-8, a disappointing three-game decline from the previous year when the team advanced to the NFC championship game, losing to Seattle. Nevertheless, Bridges had started in each of the team's 14 games from Week 3 onward, showing promise to remain as a full-time offensive lineman.

THE CRIME…

The day before the team's training camp opened in July 2007, however, Bridges was arrested after pointing a gun at a female employee of Club Onyx, a Charlotte strip club. He was released on a $3,000 bond and charged with misdemeanour assault. The incident took place during a parking lot fight outside the establishment, early in the morning.

The subsequent trial took a bizarre twist when Bridges's accuser testified that she didn't even date men. Two witnesses also took the stand to support her. One was her pregnant ex-girlfriend and another was her cross-dressing uncle who showed up wearing a sleeveless black evening dress and high-heels.

Bridges was found guilty of the charge and given a 60-day suspended sentence and one year probation. He was also ordered to perform 60 hours of community service and had to forfeit the gun. Further, Bridges was suspended for the first two games of the 2007 season for conduct detrimental to the team. Moving to the guard position after spending his career as a tackle, he started in ten of the 13 games in which he appeared that year. Carolina finished with a subpar 7-9 mark. An elbow injury to quarterback to Jake Delhomme in Week 3 had set the Panthers' fortunes back for another season.

WHAT FOLLOWED...

Throughout 2008, Bridges had been relegated to the bench, playing only sparingly. Delhomme, meanwhile, recovered from surgery on his elbow to become one of the most dangerous passers in the game. With explosive running back DeAngelo Williams on the way to a 1,515-yard season, the Panthers' offense was firing on all cylinders.

On the eve of a huge divisional matchup on Monday Night Football against rival Tampa Bay, Bridges was arrested for the second time in a 16-month span. A warrant was issued after an incident in a Charlotte restaurant called Villa Antonio. Bridges was out celebrating his anniversary with his wife when he reportedly doused several customers with Dom Perignon champagne. The manager asked the couple to leave, and Bridges obliged.

> # On the eve of a huge divisional matchup on Monday Night Football against rival Tampa Bay, Bridges was arrested for the second time in a 16-month span.

But, as reported by the *Charlotte Observer*, a woman – a customer who was sprayed during the exuberant celebration – pursued Bridges, complaining loudly. In response, Bridges reacted violently, to the point where he had to be restrained by a bouncer. He allegedly made physical contact with the bouncer, but not with any of the restaurant patrons. Bridges was charged with two misdemeanour counts of simple assault and battery and one count of communicating threats. The Panthers de-activated him from their roster the next day.

Carolina clinched the NFC South Division with a 12-5 record but was upset by Arizona in the divisional playoffs. On February 25, 2009, Bridges was released outright by the Panthers.

Bridges attended the Washington Redskins' training camp but was cut prior to the start of the regular season and signed with Arizona, where he had made his professional debut five years earlier. He played an additional three seasons with the Cardinals, appearing in all 48 regular season games, but starting in just one-third of them.

As the 2012 campaign opened, Bridges was placed on injured reserve with torn thumb ligaments. He was eventually waived on November 5 and re-signed with Carolina the following week. Bridges played a pair of games for the Panthers in his second tenure with the club but was waived again before the season ended, effectively finishing his pro career.

Did You Know...?

Bridges is one of several retired NFL players involved in the $765-million lawsuit filed against the league as a result of sustaining head injuries. Toledo lawyer Norman Abood is representing Bridges, his Arizona teammate tight end Johnny McWilliams, former Pittsburgh receiver Antwaan Randle El, and former Carolina cornerback Dante Wesley.

Abood is one of six lawyers acting on the players' behalf. Although the NFL reached a settlement with the plaintiffs in August 2013, the agreement was dismissed five months later by Judge Anita Brody.

"The judge felt she didn't have enough information about the economics of the settlement," Abood told the *Toledo Free Press.* "She saw that it was going to be appealed by us, and it's a good sign we are going to get to the meat of the problem sooner rather than later, and that's in everyone's best interest. But there's all these financial variables you have to factor in to see if there's enough money to pay all of the potential claimants."

TODD MARINOVICH

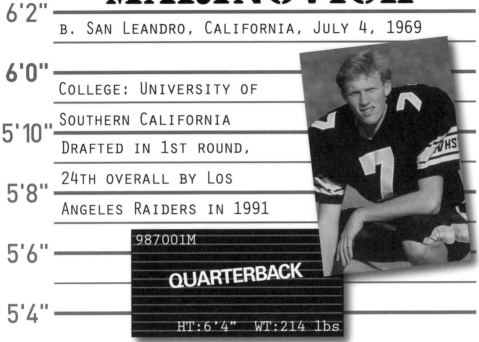

B. SAN LEANDRO, CALIFORNIA, JULY 4, 1969

COLLEGE: UNIVERSITY OF SOUTHERN CALIFORNIA

DRAFTED IN 1ST ROUND, 24TH OVERALL BY LOS ANGELES RAIDERS IN 1991

987001M

QUARTERBACK

HT:6'4" WT:214 lbs

IN THE BEGINNING...

The son of a former Oakland Raiders offensive lineman, Todd Marinovich was groomed by his father Marv to become a professional football player from a very young age. The senior Marinovich retired after a three-year professional career to become a professional sports trainer, instilling his exercise habits into his children Todd and Traci throughout their childhoods.

Todd played at quarterback on his fourth-grade Pop Warner team, the Newport Beach Cheyennes. He continued at that position from there all the way through Capistrano Valley High School where used his cannon-like left arm to break the Orange County passing record. During his senior year, Marinovich was highly recruited by NCAA Division I-A schools across the country.

Nicknamed "Robo-QB" as a result of his father's strict training regimen, the tall, left-handed redhead was in the enviable position of being able to write his own ticket. He signed his letter of intent with USC, where both of his parents had attended and where Marv had captained the football Trojans in 1962.

In 1989, Marinovich threw for 2,578 yards and 16 touchdowns, leading the Pac-10 Conference with a 62.2% completion percentage. The Trojans finished with a 9-2-1 record, defeating Michigan, 17-10, in the Rose Bowl. The following year saw Marinovich's production dip just slightly to 2,423 passing yards and 13 touchdowns, but he still had the attention of NFL scouts. The Los Angeles Raiders selected Marinovich with the 24th overall pick in 1991, nine spots before Atlanta chose future Hall of Famer Brett Favre.

With Jay Schroeder holding the number-one quarterback job in Los Angeles, Marinovich didn't start a game until the final week of the 1991 regular season. He had an impressive outing, completing 23 of 40 passes, including three touchdowns, but the Raiders lost, 27-21, to the Kansas City Chiefs, the team that also ousted them in the wild card playoff game the following week.

Marinovich started seven games in his sophomore year of 1992, passing for five touchdowns and 1,102 yards. But off the field, he had turned to heavy drug use. He'd already had a previous arrest for marijuana and cocaine possession as a college senior. As a result, the NFL required him to provide frequent urine samples. By the 1993 training camp in August, Marinovich had failed three drug tests. The once highly-touted USC superstar was out of the league.

 THE CRIME...

In the late 1990s, Marinovich attempted to resume his playing career in the CFL. He attended the Winnipeg Blue Bombers' camp in 1997 but injured his knee on the first day. Meanwhile his drug addiction worsened after he discovered heroin. He was also jailed for felony marijuana cultivation, serving three months. In 1999, Marinovich was cleared to play in the NFL again but couldn't find a team to sign him after he suffered a herniated disk. As a result, he went to the CFL's BC Lions as a third-string quarterback behind Damon Allen and Khari Jones. Marinovich never took a snap.

Throughout the early 2000s, Marinovich faced several more drug-related charges as his life became a revolving door, spinning him through the Arena Football League, the Canadian Football League, and rehab facilities. Upon his fifth drug arrest in 2005, several of his teammates from USC kept Marinovich from going to jail by helping him pay for his drug treatment.

On August 26, 2007, Marinovich was skateboarding in a prohibited area – the boardwalk of Newport Pier – in Newport Beach, California. Police discovered Marinovich with his skateboard, carrying a guitar case. The former player took off on foot and fled the scene. He was discovered in the garage of nearby home. A search also turned up a syringe, a metal spoon, and a small amount of metamphetamine.

Marinovich was charged with felony possession of a controlled substance and faced two misdemeaour counts: unauthorized possession of a hypodermic needle, and resisting arrest. He was held on a $50,000 bond.

Did You Know…?

Married with two young children and a new lease on life, Marinovich has become an artist. Even when his life was spiraling out of control with drug use several years earlier, he always had a passion for drawing and painting.

"Always doodling when I should have been paying attention in class," Marinovich told the *Associated Press*. "I kind of knew then [at an early age] that it was with that route I'd be the most happy."

Marinovich has combined sports and music into much of his work. He has sold paintings of quarterbacks Joe Montana, Terry Bradshaw, and Ken Stabler and musicians Bob Dylan, George Harrison, and Keith Richards.

In 2012, Marinovich was asked to do a portrait of Bernie Williams, the four-time World Series champion with the New York Yankees. Williams offered 100 prints for sale at $500 each, with much of the proceeds going towards benefiting a food outreach program.

"This very exciting opportunity presented itself this past season, and I was able to team up with Bernie for a great cause," Marinovich said in a news release.

In 2011, ESPN released an episode of its "30-for-30" documentary series entitled "The Marinovich Project" chronicling the ex-football player's promising career that was destroyed by addiction.

WHAT FOLLOWED…

Marinovich was given five years' probation and ordered to spend one year at the Spencer Recovery Center in Laguna Beach. In addition, he was required to go through a four-phase, court-ordered drug program and appear in court on a monthly basis. In 2009, during the second phase of the rehabilitation process, Marinovich missed a hearing and was jailed briefly.

In 2011, ESPN released an episode of its "30-for-30" documentary series entitled "The Marinovich Project" chronicling the ex-football player's promising career that was destroyed by addiction. While reviewing the episode on radio on "The Dan Patrick Show," Marinovich said he felt no animosity towards his father, who practically treated him as a science project from the time that he was born. "I don't put any blame on him at all," Marinovich said. "As I've gotten older and worked through some things, I know he did those things with love in his heart."

BRYANT McKINNIE

B. WOODBURY, NEW JERSEY, SEPTEMBER 23, 1979

COLLEGE: MIAMI (FLORIDA)

DRAFTED IN 1ST ROUND, 7TH OVERALL BY MINNESOTA IN 2002

608355M

TACKLE

HT:6'8" WT:335 lbs

6'2"
6'0"
5'10"
5'8"
5'6"
5'4"

IN THE BEGINNING…

As a student at Woodbury High School in his New Jersey hometown, Bryant McKinnie was a prodigious athlete. He not only captained the school's football team but was a track and field star in both shot put and discus. A dominating force on the offensive line, McKinnie starred for the University of Miami Hurricanes, guarding quarterback Ken Dorsey with as much diligence as a Secret Service agent would protect the President of the United States. In his junior year, 2000, the Hurricanes finished with an 11-1 record, ending their season with a Sugar Bowl win.

McKinnie punctuated his collegiate career with a bang, earning a consensus First Team All-American selection. He won the Outland Trophy as the most outstanding interior lineman in college football and also finished eighth overall in voting for the Heisman Trophy. With a dominating 37-14 performance over Nebraska in the Rose Bowl, Miami claimed the national championship. Throughout his high school and college career, McKinnie did not allow a sack. He graduated from Miami with a degree in psychology.

The Vikings selected McKinnie with the seventh-overall pick at the 2002 draft and inserted him into the lineup for the final seven games of the season. As his career evolved, McKinnie proved his durability, consistently starting in all 16 games of each year while providing protection for quarterback Daunte Culpepper and running back Adrian Peterson.

THE CRIME…

McKinnie was the only Vikings offensive player to start in all 16 games in the 2005 season. During that year, an infamous incident occurred in which several Vikings players, including McKinnie, were charged in a lewd party scandal dubbed "The Love Boat" affair (see page 99). McKinnie and teammates Fred Smoot and Moe Williams each pleaded guilty to misdemeanours, resulting in fines and community service.

Did You Know…?

Apart from his legal issues, McKinnie also faced financial hardships. In 2012, the Ravens' Super Bowl winning season, the team garnished his wages as a result of a lawsuit settlement stemming from a $4.5 million loan that McKinnie took out during that year's NFL lockout. Then, McKinnie was sued by Charles "Pop" Young, the father of rapper Trick Daddy. The plaintiff alleged that McKinnie owed $375,000 for unpaid tabs at two Miami strip clubs.

McKinnie denied the allegations. "I got no papers; I was never served," he told the *Baltimore Sun*. "I just called my lawyer about this because this is a bogus story. I just read the article. [Young] was working at those places, and he's tried to borrow money from me."

"People can put anything out there. What strip club gives you a $375,000 tab? It just sounds stupid to me. I've never heard of this in my life. This is bogus to me. I would never pay this guy because what he's saying isn't true. This is the least of my worries."

By the end of the 2007 campaign, McKinnie had played in 87 consecutive regular-season games. Minnesota's offensive line effectively cleared lanes for their powerhouse backfield tandem of Peterson and Chester Taylor as the Vikings led the NFL with 2,634 rushing yards, a team record.

Early on the morning of February 24, 2008, however, McKinnie was arrested after a brawl outside a Miami night club. He was charged with aggravated battery, disorderly conduct, and resisting arrest without violence. Police were called to Club Space where the player had been thrown out by bouncer Eric Otero. McKinnie left the premises but returned a short time later to fight Otero again.

As reported in the *Miami Herald*, McKinnie spit in Otero's face and then shoved a camera phone in his face. Otero slapped the phone out of McKinnie's hands, and the player responded by picking up a heavy pole and slamming it over the Otero's head. The action was witnessed by a large crowd who had gathered to watch the fracas. McKinnie was reportedly throwing punches and screaming profanities.

McKinnie was released on a $9,000 bond. The aggravated battery charge against him was a second-degree felony that carried a maximum penalty of 15 years in prison.

WHAT FOLLOWED...

The NFL suspended McKinnie for the first four games of the 2008 season for violation of the league's personal-conduct policy. He returned to play in the team's final twelve games as the Vikings finished at 10-6 to clinch first place in the NFC North Division. Their first playoff berth in four years ended with a wild card loss to Philadelphia.

In March 2009, McKinnie avoided a trial by agreeing to perform 25 hours of community service and take anger management classes, with the provision that he not have any further violations.

That fall, future Hall of Fame quarterback Brett Favre joined the Vikings.

The NFL suspended McKinnie for the first four games of the 2008 season for violation of the league's personal-conduct policy.

Prior to his previous one-year stint with the New York Jets, Favre enjoyed a long career with Minnesota's rivals, the Green Bay Packers. With Favre handing off to Peterson, and with Sidney Rice catching the quarterback's passes, the Vikings had one of the most potent offenses in the NFL, ranking fifth in the league in yards per game.

For the first time in his career, McKinnie was named to the Pro Bowl. Minnesota posted a 12-4 mark en route to their second consecutive division title. The Vikings advanced to the NFC championship game, losing an overtime thriller to New Orleans, the eventual Super Bowl winners.

McKinnie played with Minnesota for one more year before signing as a free agent with Baltimore in August 2011. He played in all 32 regular season games with the Ravens over a two-year stretch, winning a Super Bowl with the team at the end of the 2012 season. By the time he re-signed in the off-season, he had not missed any game due to injury in 164 consecutive regular season NFL appearances.

Midway through the 2013 campaign, McKinnie was traded to the Miami Dolphins. He replaced Jonathan Martin at left tackle after the latter left the team amid accusations that he was being bullied by teammate Richie Incognito.

BRANDON MARSHALL

6'2"

B. PITTSBURGH, PENNSYLVANIA, MARCH 23, 1984

6'0"

COLLEGE: CENTRAL FLORIDA

5'10"

DRAFTED IN 4TH ROUND,

119TH OVERALL BY DENVER

5'8"

IN 2006

5'6"

711986M

WIDE RECEIVER

5'4"

HT:6'4"   WT:229 lbs

IN THE BEGINNING...

Growing up in Winter Park, Florida, Brandon Marshall lived in a broken home, his parents having divorced when he was a young boy. He excelled in sports and was an All-State football player at Lake Howell High School, where he also lettered in basketball and track and field.

Upon graduation, Marshall went on to star in football at the University of Central Florida. He had a remarkable senior year in 2005, leading Conference USA with eleven receiving touchdowns and finishing second overall with 1,195 receiving yards. In the final game of the year, the Central Florida Knights battled the Nevada Wolf Pack in the Hawaii Bowl.

The spotlight shone on Marshall, who caught three touchdowns, including a game-tying 16-yard grab in the end zone with just 55 seconds remaining in the fourth quarter to send the game into overtime. But UCF missed an extra point in the extra session to fall 49-48 in a heartbreaking thriller. Marshall was co-winner of the game's MVP award with Wolf Pack running back B.J. Mitchell.

During his time in college, Marshall had a pair of minor run-ins with the law. On Hallowe'en in 2004, he was arrested on misdemeanour charges of trespass and assault on a police officer following an incident in which he allegedly created a disturbance at a Denny's restaurant in Orlando. The charges were later dismissed. Less than six months later, he was accused of retail theft in the amount of $20, but – once again – the charges were dropped.

When the Denver Broncos chose Marshall in the fourth round of the 2006 draft, the incidents seemed inconsequential. But in reality, the player's police blotter would only grow larger.

THE CRIME...

Two months after he was drafted into the NFL, Marshall was involved in the first of many alleged episodes of domestic abuse. On June 17, 2006, he and his then-girlfriend Rasheedah Watley filed separate police reports against each other following a heated argument, each claiming that the other was the instigator. Marshall

Did You Know...?

While Marshall has a history of problematic behaviour, the NFL picked a poor time to enforce its policies. As an advocate of mental health issues, Marshall managed to run afoul of the NFL in October 2013, but the infraction was anything but immoral. During Chicago's Week 6 game, a Thursday night tilt against the New York Giants, Marshall wore green cleats in support of Mental Health Awareness Week.

In so doing, he broke the league-sanctioned dress code for October where all players were to wear pink gloves and cleats to support Breast Cancer Awareness Month. As a result, Marshall was fined $10,500. He not only matched the fine, but also auctioned off the cleats, donating the proceeds in both instances to mental health charities.

said that Watley punched him and scratched his chest. Watley, in turn, told police that Marshall slapped her in the face and pushed her to the ground. No arrests were made.

Nine months later, Marshall was arrested for false imprisonment and domestic violence. Watley told police that she was planning to fly back to her home in Atlanta, to get away from Marshall. The couple argued at the Denver airport, but Watley eventually relented and returned to live with her partner. When Watley tried to leave a second time, Marshall blocked her taxi with his own vehicle, a Dodge Charger, and reportedly punched the cab's windows. Charges were later dropped when Marshall successfully completed an anger management program.

Marshall's string of arrests weren't limited to the allegations of violence.

Two further altercations between Marshall and Watley occurred in June 2007, but again neither resulted in the filing of any charges. Marshall was arrested again in March 2008 after three incident reports and a criminal warrant were filed after yet another fight between the couple.

Police were called to the couple's Atlanta condo where they discovered Marshall bleeding from his hand, and Watley sporting several cuts on her lips. Marshall said his hand had been cut on glass during the argument, while Watley told police that the player had also punched her in the mouth and eye. Marshall was arrested on a misdemeanour battery charge and was ordered by a subsequent restraining order to refrain from coming within 200 yards of Watley.

When training camp opened that summer, the NFL suspended Marshall for the first three games of the 2008 season for violating the league's personal-conduct policy. The ban was reduced to just one game after Marshall complied with league-mandated counseling, among other conditions. On the field, Marshall developed into one of the league's most dangerous receivers, earning the first of five Pro Bowl nominations in 2008.

In August 2009, a six-person jury acquitted Marshall on all charges stemming from the incident 17 months earlier.

WHAT FOLLOWED...

Marshall's string of arrests weren't limited to the allegations of violence. He was booked for driving under the influence in October 2007, registering a blood alcohol reading of 0.116. Eventually he received one year of probation after pleading guilty to a lesser charge of driving while ability-impaired.

His erratic behaviour can be traced to a horrifying New Year's Eve that claimed the life of one of his Denver teammates. On December 31, 2006, Marshall, along with fellow Broncos Darrent Williams and Javon Walker, were ringing in the new year at a night club. As recounted in *Sports Illustrated*, Marshall's cousin Blair Clark sprayed some of the celebrants with champagne at midnight. One of the patrons involved was a gangster known as Little Willie. Marshall and Clark exchanged verbal hostilities with Little Willie and his companions. When Little Willie was subsequently ejected from the premises, he drove alongside a limousine and opened fire. Williams was killed in the shooting.

At the ensuing trial, an entirely plausible theory surfaced, surmised by the presiding judge, that the bullets that killed Williams were intended for Marshall. Little Willie was convicted and sentenced to life in prison, plus an additional 1,152 years for 16 attempted murder charges.

In July 2011, Marshall revealed that he had been diagnosed with borderline personality disorder.

Following stops in Denver and Miami, Marshall has continued his prolific football career as a member of the Chicago Bears.

CHARLES GRANT

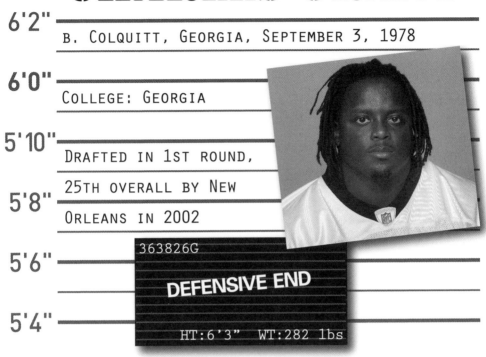

6'2"

B. COLQUITT, GEORGIA, SEPTEMBER 3, 1978

6'0"

COLLEGE: GEORGIA

5'10"

DRAFTED IN 1ST ROUND,

25TH OVERALL BY NEW

5'8"

ORLEANS IN 2002

363826G

5'6"

DEFENSIVE END

5'4"

HT:6'3"   WT:282 lbs

IN THE BEGINNING...

After starring at Miller County High School in his hometown of Colquitt, Georgia, Charles Grant forged his college career by pounding opposing quarterbacks. By graduation in 2001, he had registered 15 sacks during his time at the University of Georgia, which ended with a 20-16 defeat at the hands of Boston College in the Music City Bowl.

After being taken in the first round of the 2002 draft by New Orleans, Grant was immediately inserted into the roster on the defensive line, suiting up in each of the Saints' 16 games in his rookie season while earning six starts. The highlight of his freshman campaign was a 34-yard fumble recovery in the fourth quarter of New Orleans' Week 10 win over Carolina.

Grant evolved into the most dangerous pass rusher on his team, reaching double-digits in sacks for the Saints in each of the following two seasons. At the end of the 2004 season, Grant had 27.5 sacks to his credit, the most by any Saints player over the first three years of a career in club history.

In February 2007, Grant was designated a franchise player. Two months later, the Saints rewarded Grant by signing him to a seven-year contract with the potential to reach as much as $63 million if he attained certain bonuses. But Grant suffered an ankle injury midway through the 2007 season in a game against San Francisco. The severity of the injury was known only by the Saints coaches and upper management. He missed just two games but may have been rushed back into the lineup. Grant struggled through the season, registering just two-and-a-half sacks, but vowed to be ready for the next year.

 THE CRIME…

The New York Giants were the toast of the football world on February 3, 2008, after they upset the previously undefeated New England Patriots in Super Bowl XLII. But earlier that morning, at a night club in Blakely, Georgia, a deadly incident unfolded, making the evening's game inconsequential.

During an altercation outside a Pokie's Club, Grant was stabbed in the neck. The cut required 13 stitches to close. But the result for 23-year-old Korynda Reed was fatal. Reed, who was five months pregnant, was shot to death in the melee that officers said started inside the club and then moved outside. Reed succumbed to her injuries after being transported to Southeast Alabama Medical Center. Her unborn child did not survive.

Police described Reed as an innocent bystander who had been accidentally hit by a stray bullet. Meanwhile, Grant had been attacked after three gunshots were fired, according to police. There was no known connection between Grant and Reed.

Three months later, Grant was indicted on charges of involuntary manslaughter. An Early County grand jury also charged the man who fired the gun, Laquient

Macklin – a longtime friend of Grant – with felony murder and feticide. Five other men, including Grant's cousin, Marshae Stromer, also received involuntary manslaughter charges.

WHAT FOLLOWED...

If that wasn't enough, Grant was dealing with a slew of other issues. In December 2008, he along with teammates Deuce MacAllister and Will Smith were suspended for four games for violating the league's policy on steroids and related substances. The suspensions came as a result of positive drug tests for bumetanide, a banned diuretic, which can be used to mask the presence of steroids in the body.

Grant, who was already out for the season with a triceps injury, appealed the suspension. The three Saints players, along with two Vikings players who received similar bans for the same infraction, argued that the NFL knew bumetanide had been detected in StarCaps, a weight-loss supplement. The product, which could be purchased over the counter, did not list bumetanide as an ingredient, and the league failed to notify the players of the diuretic's presence, according to the appellants. The NFL relented, lifting the suspensions as training camps opened the following summer.

Three months after the Saints celebrated on Bourbon Street, Grant had the involuntary manslaughter charge against him dropped.

The year 2009 was a banner one for New Orleans as the Saints won the Super Bowl, defeating the Indianapolis Colts. Grant missed the playoffs after reinjuring his triceps in the final game of the regular season, but he still received a championship ring.

Three months after the Saints celebrated on Bourbon Street, Grant had the involuntary manslaughter charge against him dropped. Just before the start of the trial stemming from the horrific events of two years earlier, he agreed to plead no contest to affray (public fighting), a misdemeanour. He was fined $1,000 and given one year of unsupervised probation. He also reimbursed the Early County Sherriff's Office for the cost of the investigation: $20,000.

Macklin and Stromer both pleaded guilty to involuntary manslaughter, serving two years' probation in addition to paying $1,000 fines. Macklin admitted to firing the gun during the night club altercation, claiming self-defence against a growing mob which escalated to the point that bottles and rocks were being thrown.

Woodrow Gray, the man who stabbed Grant, pleaded guilty to aggravated assault and involuntary manslaughter. He received ten years' probation.

Grant was released by the Saints in the off-season, signing with Miami before the start of the 2010 campaign. He was cut after training camp and attempted to resume his career with Chicago. After the Bears released him two weeks later, he was out of the NFL.

Did You Know...?

After retiring from football, Grant went from making the sports pages to the entertainment tabloids. He was on romantic terms with "Real Housewives of Atlanta" star NeNe Leakes before entering into a relationship with Marlo Hampton, who made an unsuccessful attempt to become a regular cast member on the same show.

In December 2011, Grant was arrested for passing bad cheques; a felony charge since the amount written was over $500. Ex-girlfriend Hampton also had a checkered past with a rap sheet that included charges of aggravated battery and probation violation.

When news broke of Grant's brushes with the law, the opportunistic tabloids jumped in with their own jeers: "At least they have matching mug shots!"

PLAXICO BURRESS

6'2"

B. NORFOLK, VIRGINIA, AUGUST 12, 1977

6'0"

COLLEGE: MICHIGAN

STATE

5'10"

DRAFTED IN 1ST ROUND,

8TH OVERALL BY

5'8"

PITTSBURGH IN 2000

654226B

5'6"

WIDE RECEIVER

5'4"

HT:6'5"   WT:226 lbs

IN THE BEGINNING…

Plaxico Burress was a talented multi-sport athlete at Green High School in Virginia Beach, Virginia. He started on the basketball team as a small forward and also excelled at hurdles, winning a state title in the 300-metre event during his senior year.

Football, however, was his ultimate calling. Burress was named to three prep All-America teams in 1995. He moved on to have a brief but phenomenal college career playing for the Michigan State Spartans. In 1998, he caught 65 passes for 1,013 yards, ranking fifth and third in the Big Ten conference in the respective categories. He was even better the following season, taking in 66 receptions for 1,142 yards.

Burress's 12 receiving touchdowns led the Big Ten. In his final college outing, the Citrus Bowl, played on New Year's Day 2000, Burress was named the game's MVP after scoring three touchdowns in Michigan State's 37-34 win over Florida.

After being chosen in the first round of the 2000 draft by the Pittsburgh Steelers, Burress's initiation into the NFL was less than stellar. He played in 12 of 16 games and made 22 catches. But, he infamously made the blooper reels in Week 5 versus Jacksonville when he spiked the ball after making a 19-yard catch, falling to the ground without being touched by a defender.

The play would have been nothing more than a showboat celebration under college rules, but in the pro league the ball was still live. A Jaguars defender recovered the ball and ran it back for what was ruled a 44-yard fumble by Burress. Fortunately for Pittsburgh, the team held on for a 24-13 win as Burress's teammates gave him the unflattering nickname "Spike Lee."

Recovering from his mediocre freshman year, Burress played an additional four seasons in Pittsburgh. He had a career high 1,325 receiving yards in 2002, the fifth-best total in the NFL that year. After breaking off contract negotiations with the Steelers in 2005, Burress signed a six-year, $25 million deal with the New York Giants. A frequent target of quarterback Eli Manning during his time in New York, Burress twice topped the 1,000-yard mark in receiving, including the 2007 season that ended with a victory in Super Bowl XLII. Burress's 13-yard catch from Manning with 39 seconds left in the fourth quarter was the winning score in a 17-14 upset over the New England Patriots.

 THE CRIME...

Burress was rewarded with a five-year, $35 million extension prior to the start of the 2008 season. By Thanksgiving weekend, the Giants looked poised to repeat as Super Bowl champions, springing to a remarkable 10-1 record.

Shortly after 1:30am on November 29, 2008, however, Burress went to a night club in New York called Latin Quarter with teammate Antonio Pierce. Burress was carrying an illegal handgun, a .40 calibre Glock, in the waistband of his pants. As he walked to a VIP area carrying a drink in one hand, the gun started sliding

Did You Know…?

Burress's game-winning touchdown in Super Bowl XLII was preceded by a memorable, miraculous catch by teammate David Tyree, 36 seconds earlier on the late fourth-quarter drive engineered by Eli Manning.

On the play, Manning eluded the grasp of New England Patriots linemen Richard Seymour and Jarvis Green before launching a 32-yard pass that was grabbed by Tyree as he pressed the football against his helmet, barely an inch off the ground.

After the Giants' win, referee Mike Carey told the *New York Daily News* the following week that he felt that a sack – or at least grasp and control – was imminent on the play, and would have had to have blown the play dead if either defender had pushed Manning backwards.

"Boy, was it close," Carey said. "I anticipated a sack. Rarely do you see a quarterback escape when he's got that much weight on his back and being dragged by two or three guys who had a hold of him."

down his leg. When he reached for the gun, he fumbled it, and the weapon discharged, shooting him in the thigh. The bullet also narrowly missed hitting a security guard. ESPN reported that a person saw the bloody pistol fall out of Burress's pant leg and land on the floor before the player said, "Take me to a hospital."

Burress was treated at New York-Presbyterian Hospital after he checked in with a fake name – Harris Smith. When police eventually recovered the gun, they discovered that it was not licensed in New York or New Jersey, where Burress lived. Three days later, Burress was charged with two felony counts of criminal possession of a weapon in the second degree. He was booked and released on a $100,000 bond.

"We all are upset about what happened with Plaxico, and hopefully he's going to be fine and so on and so forth. That's our first concern," said Giants coach Tom Coughlin upon hearing of the incident. "Once that was taken care of, we knew that he was okay, then the guys got right back to focusing on the reason we were here."

WHAT FOLLOWED...

The New York Giants suspended Burress for the remainder of the season for conduct detrimental to the team. Meanwhile, the star receiver faced a possible three-and-a-half to 15 years in prison if convicted.

In August 2009, Burress accepted a deal in which he pleaded guilty to a lesser charge of attempted weapons possession. As a result, he received a lighter sentence of 20 months behind bars, just slightly more than half of the minimum sentence that he had been facing. Judge Michael Melkonian showed compassion by allowing Burress to say goodbye to his family who attended his sentencing hearing. At the time his wife, Tiffany, was pregnant, and his son Elijah was not yet three years old.

In August 2009, Burress accepted a deal in which he pleaded guilty to a lesser charge of attempted weapons possession.

Burress was released from jail in June 2011. After being reinstated by the NFL, he signed with the New York Jets for the 2011 season. He appeared in all of the club's 16 games – 13 as a starter – catching eight passes for touchdowns. The Jets declined to re-sign him the following year, and he wasn't picked up until November when Pittsburgh signed him, his second stint with the Steelers.

A torn rotator cuff kept Burress on the sidelines for the entire 2013 season, but he expressed a desire to continue to play in the NFL.

DAVE MEGGETT

6'2"

B. CHARLESTON, SOUTH CAROLINA, APRIL 30, 1966

6'0"

COLLEGE: MORGAN STATE,

TOWSON STATE

5'10"

DRAFTED IN 5TH ROUND,

132ND OVERALL BY NEW

5'8"

YORK GIANTS IN 1989

909286M

5'6"

RUNNING BACK /
KICK RETURNER /
PUNT RETURNER

5'4"

HT:5'7" WT:190 lbs

IN THE BEGINNING...

Just 5 feet, 7 inches tall, Dave Meggett used his explosive speed to make his impact on the gridiron. After playing cornerback at Morgan State University, Meggett transferred to Towson State where he made the transition from defence to offence, becoming a tailback and kick returner.

He made his NFL debut with the New York Giants in 1989 under coach Bill Parcells, but Meggett's first pre-season game was disastrous as the return man misplayed three punts. Parcells was unfazed. He told the *New York Times*. "I'm going to have him return punts until I can't stand it anymore."

The coach's faith in the fifth-round draft pick was well-justified. Meggett starred as a rookie, playing in all 16 games and highlighted by a 76-yard kick return for a touchdown against the Los Angeles Raiders on Christmas Eve, the longest such score in the NFL that season. Meggett's total of 528 punt-return yards led the league. The 23-year-old capped off an outstanding freshman season by being named to the Pro Bowl.

The year 1990 saw Meggett lead the league in punt-return yards once again, with a total of 467. The Giants ended the San Francisco 49ers' bid for a third straight title by upsetting them in the NFC championship game. One week later, the team was hoisting the Vince Lombardi Trophy as it defeated Buffalo in Super Bowl XXV when the Bills' Scott Norwood's field goal attempt sailed wide at the end of the game.

Coach Parcells entered into a brief retirement but resurfaced with New England two years later. Meggett played in New York until signing as a free agent with the Patriots in 1995 to play for his old mentor. In 1996, New England advanced to Super

Did You Know...?

Meggett's record of 3,708 career punt-return yards stood until it was broken by Brian Mitchell, who played for 14 years in the NFL including a decade with the Washington Redskins. Mitchell also played for three years for the Philadelphia Eagles and one year for the New York Giants. When he retired in 2003, Mitchell had compiled an astonishing 4,999 return yards on punts.

The record seems unbeatable, given that no other returner in league history has even eclipsed the 4,000-yard mark. However, the NFL's current active leader in that category, Atlanta's Devin Hester – formerly of the Chicago Bears – has compiled 3,241 punt-return yards and ranks eighth all-time as of games played at the end of 2013. He is also the league's all-time leader with 13 punt returns for touchdowns.

Going into the 2014 season, Hester, 31, has played eight NFL seasons averaging 405 punt-return yards a year. If he plays another six years to match Mitchell's career tenure, Hester would have to average 293 yards per season to break the mark. He returned punts for 256 yards in 2013, his lowest total in the past four seasons of declining numbers.

Accomplishing the feat is a longshot, but not impossible.

Bowl XXXI, losing to Green Bay. Meggett had a career-best 588 punt-return yards in the regular season and was named to the Pro Bowl for the second time in his career.

 THE CRIME…

On February 27, 1998, Meggett was arrested in Toronto on charges of sexual assault against a 33-year-old escort at the Royal York Hotel. The alleged incident occurred during a bachelor party for ex-teammate Steve Brannon, who was then playing for the CFL's Argonauts. The Crown didn't pursue the rape charge, proceeding only with assault and theft charges. Meggett's trial resulted in a hung jury, and prosecutors didn't seek a retrial.

The incident led to Meggett's release from the Patriots, in large measure because team owner Robert Kraft had no tolerance for violence against women. The player was about to enter the fourth year of a five-year contract worth more than $8 million. In December, Meggett signed with the New York Jets where he was united with coach Parcells for a third time.

Meggett retired at season's end. The return specialist had compiled 3,708 punt- return yards in his career, the most in NFL history at the time (since eclipsed by Brian Mitchell).

But the prosecution's case was strong.

But the Toronto arrest was a foreshadowing of a far more serious crime.

In 2009, Meggett was arrested and charged with raping a woman in North Charleston, South Carolina. The victim, 21-year-old Stacy Hooper, had befriended Meggett, knowing him only as "Mike," calling on him for a favour when she needed to borrow $200. Shortly after midnight on January 14, Hooper awoke to find "Mike" sitting on her bed, demanding full repayment of the debt.

When Meggett was told by Hooper that she didn't have the money, he raped her.

Meggett was denied bond. At the time of the arrest, Meggett had already been out on bond relating to a September 2008 criminal sexual conduct charge involving a 17-year-old girl, also living in North Charleston.

WHAT FOLLOWED...

Meggett's defence lawyer contended at his trial that the sex between him and Hooper was consensual, and that the two later had an argument. Beattie Butler, the defence attorney, attempted to portray Hooper as a person lacking credibility and good judgment, referring to previous consensual sex that Meggett said had taken place, prior to the alleged rape.

But the prosecution's case was strong. Meggett was said to have grabbed Hooper around her neck, holding her hand behind her back during the ordeal.

A jury convicted Meggett of first degree criminal sexual conduct and first degree burglary. Circuit Judge Kristi Harrington handed down a 30-year prison sentence, the maximum under the law. Meggett's previous history of sexual offense charges – at least five dating back to 1990 – was a factor in imposing the harsh judgment.

Stacy Hooper spoke with ABC News in Charleston about testifying during the three-day trial. "It was one of the hardest things I've ever had to do," she said. "Because it just brings up flashbacks and memories of what happened and the pain he caused me physically and emotionally. I was ecstatic about it because now he can't go out and hurt another person. That's what I wanted, him not to hurt someone else."

DONTE STALLWORTH

6'2"

B. SACRAMENTO, CALIFORNIA, NOVEMBER 10, 1980

6'0"

COLLEGE: TENNESSEE

5'10"

DRAFTED IN 1ST ROUND,

13TH OVERALL BY NEW

5'8"

ORLEANS IN 2002

314197S

5'6"

WIDE RECEIVER

5'4"

HT:6' WT:197 lbs

IN THE BEGINNING...

Donte Stallworth's versatility was evident during his years at Grant High School in Sacramento. The player starred at both the wide receiver and cornerback positions. After Stallworth was a selection on the National Recruiting Advisor All-America team, he pursued his college career at the University of Tennessee.

In his senior year of 2001, he scored eleven touchdowns, ten receiving and one on a punt return. The Volunteers advanced to the Citrus Bowl where they destroyed the Michigan Wolverines, 45-17. Twice in the game, Stallworth made catches at the one-yard line to set up Tennessee touchdowns.

Stallworth was drafted by the New Orleans Saints, a team in steady decline. The team finished with a 9-7 record in 2002, Stallworth's freshman year, then posted 8-8 marks in each of the next two seasons. By 2005, Stallworth had become the team's leading receiver, catching for 945 yards and seven touchdowns.

But the on-field product was a mess. Future Pro Bowl quarterback Drew Brees didn't arrive until the following year, and the interception-prone pivot Aaron Brooks was still leading the offence. The Saints posted an abysmal 3-13 record to end up in the basement of the NFC South Division. New Orleans fired head coach Jim Haslett, replacing him with Sean Payton, who didn't take a liking to Stallworth. As a result, the receiver was traded to the Philadelphia Eagles.

After a season in Philadelphia, Stallworth hit the jackpot in free agency. He signed a one-year, $3.6 million deal with New England in 2007. From there, it was on to Cleveland where the player was inked to a seven-year contract worth $35 million. Unfortunately, Stallworth suffered a pulled quadriceps muscle in training camp and was ineffective for much of the 2008 season, catching for just 170 yards and a single touchdown in eleven games.

 **THE CRIME…**

In the early morning of March 14, 2009, Stallworth left the Fountainebleau Miami Beach hotel after a night of drinking. When he got behind the wheel of his 2005 Bentley, his blood alcohol level was 0.126, more than one-and-a-half times the

Did You Know…?

Stallworth had a misadventure in June 2013 when he surprised his then-girlfriend with a hot-air balloon ride as a birthday present. The couple had a peaceful ride for two hours until things went awry when the balloon hit a power line while approaching for a landing.

"Literally, my butt caught on fire," Stallworth said.

Both parties suffered burns in the accident. They were airlifted to hospital where they were treated and released. Stallworth's injuries healed quickly enough in time for the Washington Redskins' training camp. But the receiver did not make the team, spending the entire 2013 season as an unsigned free agent.

"The NFL and NFL players must live with the stain that you have placed on their reputations."

legal limit in Florida. As he drove down MacArthur Causeway, a construction crane operator, 59-year-old Mario Reyes, was running across the street to catch a bus home. It was 7:15am and Reyes had just finished his night shift. Stallworth came around a bend striking Reyes, who was not at a crosswalk. The pedestrian was killed in the collision.

The police didn't initially charge Stallworth, who admitted to drinking hours earlier. A police report quoted the player – who was going 50 miles per hour in a 40 mph zone – as saying that he tried to flash his lights at Reyes to warn him of his approach. However, when blood tests came back three weeks later, an arrest warrant was filed charging Stallworth with DUI manslaughter.

The Cleveland Browns issued a statement expressing disappointment in Stallworth: "We are saddened by the circumstances that have taken place, and our thoughts and prayers go out to the family of Mario Reyes."

WHAT FOLLOWED...

Stallworth pleaded guilty to the DUI manslaughter charge on June 16, 2009. Immediately after, he was suspended by the NFL for the entire season. In a letter from NFL Commissioner Roger Goodell to Stallworth, Goodell wrote, "Your conduct endangered yourself and others, leading to the death of an innocent man. The NFL and NFL players must live with the stain that you have placed on their reputations."

In response, Stallworth said, "Obviously, I am disappointed, but, as I said previously, I accept the commissioner's decision. Regardless of the length of my suspension, I will carry the burden of Mr. Reyes's death for the rest of my life." Reyes left behind a wife and 12-year-old daughter.

As a result of a plea bargain, the player was given a 30-day jail sentence, serving 24 days before his release. Stallworth had faced 15 years in prison. In addition, Stallworth also received eight years' probation and two years of house arrest. An out-of-court financial settlement with the Reyes' family was reached.

Stallworth underwent therapy at the recommendation of the league. He was reinstated after the February 2010 Super Bowl, then had his contract immediately terminated by the Browns.

Between 2010 and 2012, Stallworth played one year each with Baltimore, Washington, and New England, but he didn't start in any game during those years. He used his free time to speak about drunk driving awareness, particularly warning younger players that they weren't invincible.

"Regardless of your situation, your personal situation, if you know that there's a chance for you to be drinking that night, just don't drive," he told the *Boston Globe*. "It's not worth it."

In February 2014, Stallworth – an unsigned free agent – gave his support to Michael Sam, a University of Missouri graduate and football player who announced that he was gay.

"He's changed the conversation about homophobia in all of sports, and for this it's no longer a question if the NFL is ready for a gay player—the NFL has to be ready. And the onus is on everyone to make sure that he is in a safe workplace," Stallworth told CBS News.

ERIC NAPOSKI

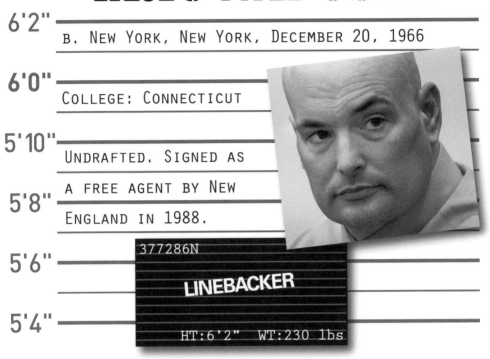

6'2"

B. NEW YORK, NEW YORK, DECEMBER 20, 1966

6'0"

COLLEGE: CONNECTICUT

5'10"

UNDRAFTED. SIGNED AS

A FREE AGENT BY NEW

5'8"

ENGLAND IN 1988.

377286N

LINEBACKER

5'6"

5'4"

HT:6'2" WT:230 lbs

IN THE BEGINNING…

Eric Naposki was a powerful linebacker and running back at Eastchester High School in New York, landing a football scholarship to attend the University of Connecticut. During his time with the U of C Huskies, Naposki clashed with coach Tom Jackson, claiming that he was demoted due to an injury. As a result, the player quit the team midway through his junior season of 1986.

Naposki made it to the roster of the New England Patriots as a walk-on tryout in 1988, appearing in three games. During the team's victory over Indianapolis on October 2, he injured his ribs, sidelining him for the year. After that, his NFL career never took flight. He played one game for the Patriots in 1989 before signing with the division rival Colts. The next year he was cut from the Cowboys' training camp after signing with Dallas as a free agent.

From there, Naposki headed across the Atlantic to play two seasons for the

Barcelona Dragons of the World League of American Football until 1992. When the WLAF (or "the Laugh," as the financially-strapped league was called by its critics) suspended operations the next year, Naposki moved to back to the U.S., settling in Orange County, California. He began his own private security business, working as a bodyguard.

THE CRIME...

In the summer of 1994, Naposki became romantically involved with Nanette Johnston, a divorced mother of two. Johnston, a gorgeous 28-year-old blonde, was already living with Bill McLaughlin, 55, a multi-millionaire and entrepreneur.

Naposki found employment as a night club bouncer not far from where McLaughlin and Johnston lived. McLaughlin had been seeing Johnston for three years and had named her a beneficiary on a million-dollar life insurance policy in his name while also including her in his will. Throughout 1994, Johnston started embezzling funds from her live-in boyfriend, writing over $350,000 in cheques payable to herself. The love triangle was about to turn deadly.

On December 15, 1994, McLaughlin arrived in Orange County from Las Vegas, arriving by his small plane and settling into his Newport Beach home. Shortly after 9pm, an intruder opened McLaughlin's front door with a key, found the homeowner, and shot his victim six times in the chest. McLaughlin was dead on the spot, lying in a pool of blood. He was discovered by his son Kevin, 24, who was upstairs at the time of the shooting.

An immediate investigation focused on Naposki and Johnston, but the pair seemed to have air-tight alibis. They were a 40-minute drive away from Newport Beach, watching Johnston's son play soccer. Johnston then left the game to go Christmas shopping while Naposki stayed to watch the rest of the game.

Johnston corroborated her own story with several mall receipts, and residue tests for gunpowder on her hands came back negative.

The circumstantial evidence against Naposki was significant, though. Naposki admitted to once owning a 9mm pistol, the same type of weapon that was used to kill McLaughlin. Police also traced the making of a new house key for McLaughlin's home to a hardware store near Naposki's residence, where the manager recognized the football player. As well, investigators drove the route to the soccer field and estimated the driving time at 40 minutes, which left plenty of time to commit the murder.

Despite the circumstantial evidence, police didn't have enough of a case to charge either Naposki or Johnston. The case remained cold for a decade-and-a-half.

Did You Know…?

The World League of American Football was established as an initiative to introduce the sport to a global audience. Ten cities were granted inaugural franchises in North America and Europe when play began in 1991. The fledgling league was supported by the NFL, which provided the WLAF with many young prospects. Games were played between April and June.

Naposki won a World Bowl with the 1997 Barcelona Dragons, a team that had Jon Kitna at quarterback. After the season, Kitna, a native of Tacoma, Washington, returned to the United States, signing with his hometown Seattle Seahawks as an unsigned free agent.

Kitna went on to have a 16-year NFL career playing in Seattle, Cincinnati, Detroit, and Dallas. He passed for 29,745 career yards and threw for 169 touchdowns, ranking 41st and 61st on the league's all-time list in those respective categories.

Late in 2013, Dallas quarterback Tony Romo suffered a season-ending back injury. Kitna – who was two years into his retirement – signed with the Cowboys to back up Kyle Orton for the team's final regular season game. Dallas lost to Philadelphia, but the signing benefited Lincoln High School in Tacoma where Kitna coached. The NFL alumnus donated his earnings from the one-game appearance, $53,000, to the school. Kitna's son Jordan was the football team's quarterback.

Coincidentally, the Cowboys' coach Jason Garrett also played in the WLAF, quarterbacking the San Antonio Riders in 1991.

WHAT FOLLOWED...

Johnston continued to steal from McLaughlin's accounts. A year after the murder she was charged with 16 counts of forgery and grand theft. In a bargain, she pleaded guilty to two counts and was given a one-year jail sentence, stayed upon completion of five years' probation.

Naposki returned to Barcelona in 1996 after the WLAF was re-launched. In 1997, the Dragons won the championship – the World Bowl. Naposki then retired from football and returned to Connecticut where he joined the coaching staff at the University of New Haven.

By 2009, both Naposki and Johnston were living their own normal, suburban lives, integrated into their respective communities as if the events that took place fifteen years earlier had never occurred. Johnston was remarried and living in Ladera Ranch as Nanette Packard, while Naposki – now working as a personal trainer in New York – was engaged.

Back in California, prosecutors reopened the McLaughlin cold case. After playing a taped conversation of a phone tip that was offered two months after the murder, an investigator tracked down the source of the tip – a man named Robert Cottrill.

Cottrill said that he placed the call after recognizing Naposki and Packard, who he had met at the gym about a month before the murder, and who he had engaged as potential investors in his software company. When Cottrill later saw the couple's faces in the news, he and his wife phoned police.

Naposki and Packard were both arrested and charged with killing McLaughlin. Each was subsequently convicted of the murder.

On May 18, 2012, Packard, was sentenced to life in prison with no possibility of parole. Three months later, Naposki was handed the same sentence.

LANCE LOUIS

6'2"
B. NEW ORLEANS, LOUISIANA, APRIL 24, 1985

6'0"
COLLEGE: SAN DIEGO STATE

5'10"
DRAFTED IN 7TH ROUND,

246TH OVERALL BY CHICAGO
5'8"
IN 2009

5'6"
277118L

GUARD

5'4"
HT:6'2" WT:303 lbs

IN THE BEGINNING…

Raised by a single mother in the West Bank of New Orleans, Lance Louis was mentored at L.B. Landry High School by coach Skip LaMothe. Under the demanding coach, players adhered to strict dress codes on game day, while LaMothe ensured that they kept their academic performances high. Louis was a top prospect at tight end as he explored his several college options, eventually choosing San Diego State University.

Louis played for two seasons at tight end for the Aztecs. His 2005 season was curtailed for four games due to injury, and he missed the entire 2006 campaign while recovering from knee surgery after tearing his ACL. The next year, Louis made the move to the offensive line where his coach Chuck Long thought he would be better suited.

"I felt it was a move to help the team," Louis told the New Orleans *Times-*

Did You Know...?

Louis grew up without a male role model. His father left the family home when the son was ten years old, leaving a mother to raise Louis and his two younger sisters. In addition, Louis's family suffered through adversity after enduring the devastation of Hurricane Katrina in August 2005. The disaster struck New Orleans while Louis was in college at San Diego State.

"When the storm came in, I wasn't able to get in touch with my family," he told the *Chicago Sun-Times*. It wasn't until three weeks later that Louis finally heard from his mother, who was in San Antonio with Louis's two sisters, aunt, and grandmother. They stayed in Texas where they had food and shelter, Louis providing whatever money he could from California.

When they finally united back home during the winter break, the remnants of the catastrophe were still evident. "New Orleans was dead and depressing," Louis said.

In Week 2 of the 2011 season, Louis returned to his hometown as the Bears visited the New Orleans at the Louisiana (now Mercedez-Benz) Superdome. The stadium, which once sheltered thousands of people seeking refuge from Hurricane Katrina and suffered massive damage in the storm, was once again a vibrant location for citizens to gather, particularly following the Saints' march to a victory in Super Bowl XLIV, two years prior.

The Bears lost, 30-13, in Louis's homecoming game.

Picayune. "I was still capable of playing tight end, but I just wanted to play. They could have told me I was the kicker."

The transition paid off as the Chicago Bears made Louis a late-round draft choice in 2009 just as teams were enquiring to see if he was interested in signing as a free agent. "I can play multiple positions, and I can play special teams," Louis said. "You can put me anywhere; I can do it. I don't worry about being a seventh-round pick."

THE CRIME...

As training camp got underway in August 2009, the *San Diego Union-Tribune* reported that Louis was under investigation for felony battery involving one of his San Diego State teammates. According to a police report, Louis allegedly attacked Nick Sandford during a team meeting on November 5, 2008. Sandford suffered a fractured cheekbone, broken eardrum, and concussion in the altercation.

Nick Sandford's father Paul said that Louis hit his son because of a disagreement that occurred earlier that day. Nick had been playing a game in the team's locker room involving a stick and ball and prodded Louis's rear end with the stick to try and get him out of harm's way, a gesture to which Louis took offense.

Compounding matters, the elder Sandford accused coach Chuck Long of being a bystander. "The head coach of a Division I university did absolutely nothing about it. Nothing. I'm angry about it," said Paul Sandford. Nick Sandford missed the team's final three games of the 2008 season, games in which Louis appeared as a starter.

Paul Sandford was told by Long that the team couldn't afford to suspend Louis because the absence of one of its key blockers would endanger the quarterback. Also, Louis's ranking at the draft would be jeopardized, the coach said.

The incident wasn't reported until November 20. Long was fired as the Aztecs' coach two days later. Meanwhile, the Bears maintained that they knew of the incident at the time they drafted Louis.

Paul Sandford was told by Long that the team couldn't afford to suspend Louis because the absence of one of its key blockers would endanger the quarterback.

WHAT FOLLOWED...

Louis played in three of Chicago's pre-season games and made the Bears' 53-man roster coming out of the 2009 training camp. He was inactive for the team's first four games of the regular season while Chicago posted a 3-1 record to start the year.

On October 13, Louis was charged with misdemeanour assault as a result of the incident. The maximum penalty that he faced was a $10,000 fine and one year in jail. He was not required to attend his arraignment, which took place ten days later in San Diego.

For the rest of Louis's rookie season, he did not step onto the football field despite dressing for three games. The Bears limped to a 7-9 record, failing to make the playoffs.

In March 2010, Louis pleaded guilty to the charge. He was sentenced to 40 hours of community service and ordered to attend anger management classes. In addition, he was given three years' probation and fined $565 as part of the plea bargain.

Louis played in all 16 games for the Bears in 2010, making four starts. The following year he switched to the defensive side of the ball as a tackle for the last eleven games of the season. He moved back to guard in 2012, starting in eleven games before suffering a season-ending injury resulting from a blindside hit by Minnesota defensive end Jared Allen. While Allen thought his hit was clean, the NFL disagreed and fined him $21,000.

In 2013, Louis was signed by Miami, but he did not make the roster and sat out for the entire year. On January 15, 2014, he was signed by Indianapolis to a reserve-future deal.

JERMAINE PHILLIPS

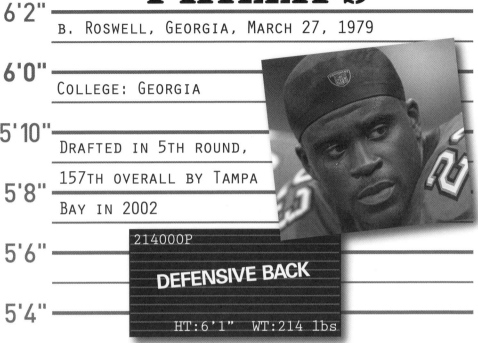

6'2"

B. ROSWELL, GEORGIA, MARCH 27, 1979

6'0"

COLLEGE: GEORGIA

5'10"

DRAFTED IN 5TH ROUND, 157TH OVERALL BY TAMPA BAY IN 2002

5'8"

214000P

DEFENSIVE BACK

5'6"

5'4"

HT:6'1" WT:214 lbs

IN THE BEGINNING...

A gifted athlete, Jermaine Phillips excelled at both basketball and football while attending Roswell High School in his Georgia hometown. In 1997, he was a starting forward on the basketball team that won the state championship, driving 100 miles south to Macon for the title-clinching game. But it was his greater skill at catching the pigskin that led Phillips to the University of Georgia. In 1999, he caught 18 passes for 235 yards and a touchdown, then switched from wide receiver to defensive back the next season.

When training camp opened in his senior year, 2001, Philips ran a mile-and-a-half in just 7 minutes and 27 seconds, the fastest time on the team and more than a minute faster than his closest competitor. He closed out his collegiate career by leading the Southeastern Conference with 89 interception return yards, picking off three passes (one for a touchdown).

The timing for Phillips couldn't have been better after the Tampa Bay Buccaneers made him a draft choice in 2002. Tampa Bay was a team on the rise after acquiring coach Jon Gruden in a trade with the Oakland Raiders. Phillips was the only rookie to play in each of the team's 16 games that season, and he was used primarily on special teams. The Buccaneers rolled to a 12-4 record to win the NFC South Division. The dream season ended with a Tampa Bay win over Gruden's former team, Oakland, in Super Bowl XXXVII. Phillips made one tackle in the Buccaneers' 48-21 victory.

Phillips made the move to free safety in his sophomore NFL season. A hard hitter with the speed to complement his physical game, Phillips had an eight-year career with Tampa Bay, playing in all five of the team's playoff games between 2002 and 2007. The only touchdown of his career came in 2008, a 38-yard fumble recovery into the end zone in Week 4 against Green Bay. In 2009, he was set to make another positional switch, from safety to linebacker, but a fractured thumb cut his season short after just two games.

THE CRIME...

An argument between Phillips and his wife of almost a year, the former Adrianne Sherman, turned violent during the morning of January 10, 2010. Philips woke his wife just after 4:30am to inquire about a number he had found on her cell phone. As the discussion escalated, Phillips choked his wife. She promptly left their home saying that she was going to walk the dog.

Police arrived on the scene, and Phillips said he pushed his wife's neck with his right hand. Phillips was arrested and charged with domestic battery by strangulation. He was held without bond.

"The Buccaneers are aware of the serious charges against Jermaine Phillips and will monitor the situation closely," said the team in a media release.

WHAT FOLLOWED...

Two months later, just days after Phillips became an unrestricted free agent, the charge against him was reduced from a felony to a misdemeanour of simple battery. In April 2010, the case against Phillips was closed, and the charge dropped, after he completed a court-ordered diversion program for domestic violence intervention. The classes were administered through the Salvation Army.

In the fall of 2010, Phillips signed with the Omaha Nighthawks of the United Football League, where he joined former Buccaneers teammates, quarterback Jeff

Did You Know...?

Phillips's ascent up the Tampa Bay depth chart came with added pressure given that he was all but asked to succeed a player who had become a cornerstone of the Buccaneers' secondary.

Safety John Lynch, an integral part of Tampa Bay's Super Bowl-winning team, was released after the 2003 season following an eleven-year career with the team that drafted him. He had five Pro Bowls to his credit at the time that the Buccaneers cut him loose. Lynch had strong ties to the city of Tampa Bay and is still revered as one of the most important athletes in the city's history. Phillips phoned Lynch before NFL training camps opened in 2004. Lynch had signed with the Denver Broncos.

"I was excited by the confidence they were showing in me, but at the same time I hated to see a guy like John Lynch leave the team and leave his legacy. He was a big part of Bucs history," Philips told the *Orlando Sentinel*.

Coach Jon Gruden reminded Buccaneers fans that Phillips had his own skill set to bring to the table. "I don't think you talk about Jermaine Phillips as John Lynch's replacement," he said. "I think you talk about Jermaine, the football player. He's a completely different kind of player. He'll put his own spin on the position."

Lynch played the last four seasons of his career in Denver, earning a Pro Bowl nomination in every year from 2004-2007. In 224 career games, Lynch made 26 interceptions and 740 solo tackles.

He was one of 15 finalists nominated for selection into the Pro Football Hall of Fame's class of 2014 but did not make the cut.

Garcia and wide receiver Michael Clayton. The next year he joined the UFL's Sacramento Mountain Lions for what turned out to be his final pro football season.

In 96 career NFL regular season games, Phillips intercepted eleven balls for 160 yards and made 338 solo tackles.

In an article Phillips wrote for the *Atlanta Journal-Constitution* on February 8, 2014, he reflected on his championship-winning team—not the Buccaneers with whom he won the Super Bowl in his rookie year, but his senior high school basketball team.

"What made that team special is that we weren't just playing for us, but for the city. How can you play for your city if you haven't been a part of it?" Phillips asked.

"Our fans had that sense of, 'he's from where I'm from,'" he continued. "Our fans saw us grow. I think that's what made that team important."

"I was excited by the confidence they were showing in me, but at the same time I hated to see a guy like John Lynch leave the team and leave his legacy."

SHAUN ROGERS

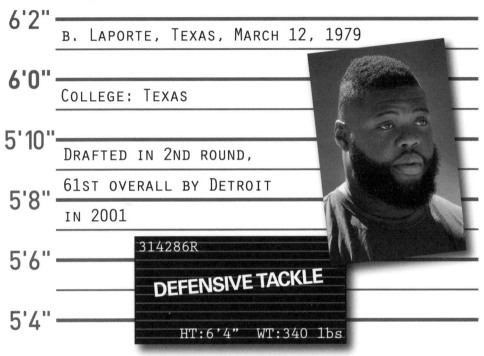

6'2"

B. LAPORTE, TEXAS, MARCH 12, 1979

6'0"

COLLEGE: TEXAS

5'10"

DRAFTED IN 2ND ROUND,

61ST OVERALL BY DETROIT

5'8"

IN 2001

5'6"

314286R

DEFENSIVE TACKLE

5'4"

HT:6'4" WT:340 lbs

IN THE BEGINNING...

With a huge exterior to mask a childlike, congenial personality, Shaun Rogers earned the nickname "Big Baby." Used primarily as a defensive tackle while playing at La Porte High School in Texas, Rogers was also occasionally utilized as a running back for short-yardage situations near the goal line. Away from the gridiron, Rogers displayed his other talents by lettering in basketball.

Many colleges recruited Rogers, and it appeared that Colorado had the inside track after it signed one of Rogers's high school teammates, Chris Anderson. But Rogers chose to attend the University of Texas, where he became one of the greatest defensive linemen in Longhorns history.

Lining up alongside tackle Casey Hampton, Rogers and his teammate formed one of the most feared tackling duos in the conference. In his junior year, 1999, Rogers recorded five-and-a-half sacks, making 27 tackles behind the line of scrimmage. He was named a First-Team All-Big 12 player that season as Texas finished with a 9-5 record, losing to Arkansas in the Cotton Bowl.

Rogers was an instant presence on Detroit's defensive line after the Lions chose him in the second round of the 2001 draft. As a rookie, he made 63 tackles and three sacks while forcing a pair of fumbles. He had incredible speed to complement his massive size, once running a 40-yard dash in 5.3 seconds.

Rogers was recognized for his stalwart play with consecutive Pro Bowl nominations in 2004 and 2005. His career had a slight setback in 2006 when he was suspended for four games for violating the NFL's steroids and related substances abuse policy. He had tested positive for the banned dietary supplement, ephedrine, which was contained in an appetite suppressant he had been taking to combat sleep apnea.

Did You Know…?

As if the ailment that derailed Rogers's 2012 season wasn't bad enough, he suffered more bad news the following March. While partying at Club Liv in Miami, Rogers met a 25-year-old woman named Subhanna Beyah. He brought her back to his room at the Fountainebleau hotel, placing his jewelry in a safe in his room.

When Rogers awoke just after noon the next day, Beyah and the jewellery were gone. The safe had been slammed shut, and hotel security was summoned to pry it open. The missing items included a pair of watches, a gold necklace, and diamond earrings. The estimated value of the theft was about $400,000.

Beyah was arrested in June 2013 in Queens, New York, on fugitive-from-justice charges. She was on the run after being pursued by authorities for multiple thefts involving jewellery and cash. However, Rogers reportedly refused to cooperate with prosecutors. As a result, the Miami-Dade State Attorney Office could not pursue the grand theft charges.

Beyah, known to police as "Crystal," is believed to be part of a ring of four women in their twenties who target unsuspecting male victims by meeting them in bars, drugging them, and stealing their valuables. One of her latest alleged victims wass a 61-year-old oil tycoon, Thomas Morgan, listed by Forbes.com as the founder of Morgan Energy.

In 2007, Rogers had an impressive first half of the year, including earning NFC defensive player of the week honours after he returned a 66-yard interception for a touchdown in Week 9 against Denver. But he fizzled throughout the rest of the season. As a result, the Lions traded him to the Cleveland Browns, where Rogers promptly signed a six-year, $42 million contract. Despite a rift between the player and coach Eric Mangini, Rogers made it to a third career Pro Bowl with his new team.

THE CRIME...

Rogers started the first eleven games of the 2009 season – his second campaign with the Browns – but was forced to the sidelines after suffering a leg injury against Cincinnati on November 29. An already decimated Cleveland team had won only a single game at the time that Rogers was lost for the remainder of year. After losing to San Diego in their 12th game, the Browns miraculously won their last four games to gain a morsel of redemption.

On April 1, 2010, Rogers was arrested at Cleveland's Hopkins International Airport after security guards found a loaded .45 calibre handgun in his carry-on luggage. He was taken into custody and booked for carrying a concealed weapon, a third-degree felony. Rogers spent the night in jail before being released the following morning.

Rogers maintained that he forgot that he was carrying the weapon. Cleveland Browns president Mike Holmgren issued a statement: "We will continue to gather additional information, and until the legal process has taken its course, we will reserve any further comment."

WHAT FOLLOWED...

Three months after the arrest, Rogers entered a diversion program to avoid a trial. Under the terms of the deal, the felony charge would be dismissed if Rogers completed 40 hours of volunteer service plus ten hours in a gun class. He was also required to forfeit the handgun.

As the 2010 season was about to get underway, there was speculation that Rogers may be suspended for violating the NFL's personal-conduct policy as a result of the incident. But the league instead chose to fine Rogers for one game's salary. The penalty amounted to about $400,000, or one-seventeenth of Rogers' $6.9 million paycheque.

Three months after the arrest, Rogers entered a diversion program to avoid a trial.

Commissioner Roger Goodell's decision not to suspend Rogers may have been influenced by the player's act of goodwill that occurred just days after he entered his July plea deal. The player phoned police to report a motorist on the highway suspected of drunk driving. He followed the erratic driver until the car in front pulled over. Rogers parked behind the offending vehicle and flashed his emergency lights to warn other motorists while waiting for police to arrive. Officers applauded his efforts.

In 2011, Rogers signed as a free agent with New Orleans. From there, he joined the Giants, intending to play the 2012 season in New York. However, a blood clot in his left calf sidelined him for the entire year. He returned the next season to play in seven games – two as a starter – making seven solo tackles.

PAT McAFEE

6'2"

B. PLUM, PENNSYLVANIA, MAY 2, 1987

6'0"

COLLEGE: WEST VIRGINIA

5'10"

DRAFTED IN 7TH ROUND,

222ND OVERALL BY

5'8"

INDIANAPOLIS IN 2009

228173M

5'6"

KICKER

5'4"

HT:5'11"   WT:228 lbs

IN THE BEGINNING...

Throughout his college career, Pat McAfee was one of the most consistently accurate kickers in the NCAA while donning the blue and gold colours of the West Virginia Mountaineers. In each of his four seasons from 2005-2008 – all ending in Bowl victories – McAfee was in the top five in the Big East conference in field goals made and field goals attempted.

In both 2006 and 2007, he led the entire NCAA in extra points made, converting all 62 point-after touchdown attempts in the former year. McAfee's career mark is 210 extra points converted. He also led the conference with a career average of 43.7 yards per punt over that same time period.

After being drafted by the Indianapolis Colts in 2009, McAfee earned a roster spot as a punter. The placekicker job was held by veteran Adam Vinatieri, the ex-Patriot and two-time Pro Bowler who also had a pair of Super Bowl-winning field goals for New England to his credit.

The Colts were guided by MVP quarterback Peyton Manning who led the team to the NFL's best record at 14-2. Indianapolis advanced to Super Bowl XLIV before losing, 31-17, to the New Orleans Saints. McAfee made all of the team's punts in his freshman year, average 44.3 yards per kick over the regular season.

THE CRIME...

In 2010 the Colts got off to a 4-2 start heading into their bye week. Over the first six games of the year, McAfee maintained his yards per punt average with a mark of 44.7 over 24 punts.

Just before 5:00am on October 20, 2010, McAfee was arrested in the Broad

Did You Know...?

In the world of prevailing social media, McAfee has taken to an active use of Twitter. The player has more than 189,000 followers. His use of the instant update medium has been very liberal, and in some cases, a little bit too revealing.

The night before his early morning drunken swim, McAfee tweeted "Bye week bye week bye week. Time to get some ish done. Happy Tuesday Party people."

In 2012, McAfee used 140 characters at a time to provide live updates of a Las Vegas trip in which he and his entourage gambled, drank heavily, and attended a party where hookers and heroine were present. "I'd do heroine, too, I guess, if I took things on and in places she does," read one tweet.

Despite providing perhaps 'too much information' in his updates, McAfee didn't run afoul of Colts management until January 2014 when he posted a locker room photo on Twitter in which quarterback Andrew Luck was in the background, completely nude. Somewhat fortunately, a cell phone in the foreground was held at such an angle to obscure Luck's manhood.

McAfee later apologized profusely to his teammate. The Colts fined McAfee an undisclosed amount of money. The player appeared on a radio show saying that the hit to his wallet was $10,000.

Ripple neighbourhood of Indianapolis, a trendy area of the city known for its nightlife. The player had taken a swim in a city canal in which the water temperatures were close to freezing. Police were called to the scene near the intersection of Broad Ripple Avenue and North College Avenue after a motorist – who was stopped at a red light – reported a shirtless man approaching her car. Fearing for her safety, she ran the traffic signal and called 911.

McAfee, who was soaking wet, was cooperative, concise, and honest in his response to police queries, to the point of self-incrimination. According to the *Associated Press*, when asked if he were swimming in the canal, McAfee said, "I'm not sure." When asked where his shirt was, McAfee replied, "In the water." And, when asked how much he'd been drinking, McAfee answered, "A lot, 'cause I'm drunk."

Throughout the conversation, McAfee's speech was slurred and his eyes were bloodshot. The player was so intoxicated that he needed to be propped up by police who administered a blood alcohol test. McAfee's reading was 0.15, nearly twice the legal limit for driving in Indiana. He was held in custody for about six hours before being released.

Colts president Bill Polian issued a statement through the media. "We are in the process of gathering the relevant facts," Polian said. "When that task is complete, we will deal immediately with the issue of club discipline."

WHAT FOLLOWED...

The team suspended McAfee for its Week 7 game against AFC South division rival Houston. Backup punter Jeremy Kapinos filled in nicely, averaging 44.5 yards per kick as the Colts won, 30-17.

McAfee was charged with public intoxication, a misdemenaour that carried a maximum penalty of 180 days in jail and a $1,000 fine. One month later, he entered into a diversion agreement to avoid a trial. He paid a $298 fine and was ordered to perform eight hours of community service. In addition, he was required to participate in a league-mandated alcohol awareness program.

The incident was a public relations fiasco for the Colts as McAfee was the team's fourth player in ten months to be subjected to an alcohol-related arrest. Receiver Taj Smith had been cited for drunk driving in January; defensive lineman John Gill was arrested for public intoxication after being found inebriated, lying in a ditch outside of a strip club, by police in August; and, defensive tackle Fili Moala was arrested for drunk driving in September.

McAfee has since managed to stay out of legal trouble and has continued to consistently perform on the field on the strength of his punting leg. As of the end of the 2013 season, his career average of 45.5 yards per punt ranks 12th on the NFL's all-time list.

In 2013, McAfee and his father Tim formed a non-profit organization, the Pat McAfee Foundation, to provide scholarship assistance to children of U.S. military personnel.

The incident was a public relations fiasco for the Colts as McAfee was the team's fourth player in ten months to be subjected to an alcohol-related arrest.

WILL SMITH

6'2" — b. New York, New York, July 4, 1981

6'0" — College: Ohio State

5'10" — Drafted in 1st round,

18th overall by New

5'8" — Orleans in 2004

556276S

DEFENSIVE END

HT:6'3"   WT:282 lbs

5'6"

5'4"

IN THE BEGINNING…

One of the most dominant defenders to ever wear the fleur-de-lis of the New Orleans Saints, Will Smith terrorized opposing quarterbacks at Proctor High School in his hometown of Utica, New York early in his career. He was named a high school All-American and was a selection to the Football New York All-State team.

After graduating, Smith took his talents to Ohio State University where he was just as impressive. In 2002, the Buckeyes went undefeated on the way to a national championship, upsetting Miami, 31-24, in the Fiesta Bowl. The next season, Smith – a senior – was named the Big Ten conference's defensive player of the year and defensive lineman of the year. In three seasons with Ohio State, Smith made 111 solo tackles, while his total of 21 sacks was the fifth-highest in the school's history by the time he was drafted into the NFL by the Saints.

Smith was credited with 32 solo tackles and seven-and-a-half sacks in his freshman year with New Orleans. He appeared in all 16 games as a rookie in 2004, and by his sophomore season, coach Jim Haslett rewarded his protégé by granting Smith more starts.

The Pro Bowl came calling in 2006, Smith's third season, after the player had a productive campaign in which he earned 10.5 sacks, starting in all but two of the team's games. The year was a remarkable turnaround for the Saints. It was the first season under coach Sean Payton, and free-agent signing Drew Brees led the way at quarterback. The team improved by seven wins from its previous, regrettable season to finish at 10-6, making the playoffs for the first time in six years.

"I feel bad for my husband who is innocent in all of this and all my family. I love you @iwillsmith!"

By 2009, the Saints were a top contender, and Smith had his best statistical year with 13 sacks, the second-best total among NFC defenders. New Orleans marched its way to the top seed in the conference, then ran the table in the playoffs, defeating Indianapolis, 31-17, to win Super Bowl XLIV.

 THE CRIME...

On Thanksgiving Day 2010, the Saints headed into Dallas where they spoiled the holiday festivities for Cowboys fans, defeating the home team, 30-27. Smith had an outstanding game with one sack and an interception, and New Orleans improved to 8-3 on the season.

Two days later, on November 27, Smith was arrested and charged with domestic abuse battery against his wife, Racquel. He was also charged with public intoxication. At around 2am police officers spotted the couple arguing as they left a night club. Smith was said to have grabbed his wife's hair, pulling her down the street. The Lafayette Police Department issued a statement saying that Racquel Smith sustained minor injuries in the incident. After his booking, Smith was released on a $1,000 bond.

The battery charge came with a maximum penalty of $1,000 and six months in jail. Racquel Smith took to Twitter to defend her husband. "Please allow the legal system to take its course," she said. "I feel bad for my husband who is innocent in all of this and all my family. I love you @iwillsmith!"

Did You Know...?

Smith was one of several Saints players who were initially suspended by NFL Commissioner Roger Goodell in the team's infamous bounty scandal. It was alleged that between 2009 and 2011, several defensive New Orleans players placed illegal bounties on member of opposing teams, rewarding hits that caused injury with financial bonuses.

Coach Sean Payton received a one-year ban which represented the entire 2012 season. Former defensive coordinator Gregg Williams was handed an indefinite suspension.

On the players' side, Jonathan Vilma – who was said to have placed a $10,000 bounty on Minnesota quarterback Brett Favre prior to the 2009 NFC championship game – was also suspended for the entire year. Jonathan Hargove got eight games, Scott Fujita received three games, and Smith was handed a four-game penalty.

But upon a players' appeal, Goodell appointed the man he succeeded as NFL Commissioner in 2006 – Paul Tagliabue – to preside over the proceedings. Tagliabue affirmed the existence of the Saints' bounty program, but, in the end, he decided to overturn the suspensions that had been issued by Goodell to all four players.

The ruling did not affect the suspensions handed down to either Payton or Williams.

WHAT FOLLOWED...

Smith didn't miss any playing time as a result of the arrest, and the Saints finished the season with an 11-5 record. However, the team's quest to win a second consecutive Super Bowl was halted in the first week of the playoffs after a wild card loss to Seattle.

A month later, in March 2011, Smith was indicted by a grand jury on the charges. It took a year for the player to redeem himself in the eyes of the law, but twelve months later, the charges were dismissed after Smith underwent counseling and performed community service.

The player worked more than 60 hours serving causes such as food banks and hospitals while attending 26 weeks of domestic violence counseling. "He did more than we expected," Assistant District Attorney Janet Perrodin told the *Baton Rouge Advocate*. Noting that Smith had no history of violence, Perrodin outlined the facts of the 2010 incident. "He didn't strike her with a fist. He didn't slap her. He didn't kick her. He didn't drag her down the street. She had no injuries," Perrodin said.

Smith extended an olive branch to the arresting officers. "I wish to apologize to any of the officers who were offended by my words," he said. "I do a lot of volunteer work with law enforcement officers in the New Orleans area and respect the difficult job officers do."

By the end of the 2012 season, Smith's 67.5 career sacks ranked him fourth on the Saints' all-time list since the statistic was first recorded in 1982. The player missed the entire 2013 campaign with a torn ACL. In February 2014, the club released Smith as a cost-cutting measure, saving the team $11.5 million in salary cap space.

EVERSON GRIFFEN

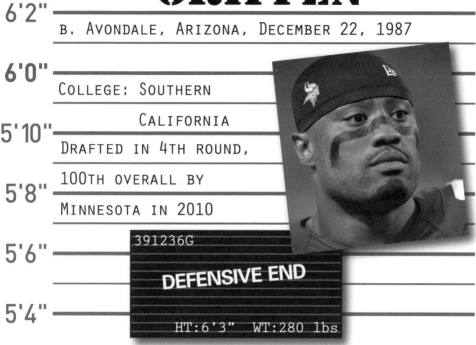

6'2"

B. AVONDALE, ARIZONA, DECEMBER 22, 1987

6'0"

COLLEGE: SOUTHERN

CALIFORNIA

5'10"

DRAFTED IN 4TH ROUND,

100TH OVERALL BY

5'8"

MINNESOTA IN 2010

391236G

DEFENSIVE END

5'6"

5'4"

HT:6'3"   WT:280 lbs

IN THE BEGINNING...

Everson Griffen excelled on both sides of the football while at Agua Fria High School in his hometown of Avondale, Arizona. From the backfield, he ran for 1,259 yards for 20 touchdowns, averaging a whopping 7.9 yards per carry in 2006, his senior year. That same season, Griffen recorded 77 tackles and 16 sacks at defensive end. For his efforts, he was recognized as an All-American by several media outlets.

After high school, Griffen took his talents to the University of Southern California where he earned a spot as a starter on the defensive line as a true – instead of redshirted – freshman. The feat hadn't been accomplished at USC since 2001 when true rookie Shaun Cody started in a game for the Trojans.

Griffen lived up to the hype, earning accolades as the Pac-10 Conference defensive player of the year as named by *The Sporting News*. He was also named to the Football Writers Freshman All-American first team. Led by coach Pete Carroll, USC rolled over Illinois, 49-17, in the Rose Bowl, ending the season as the third-ranked college team in the country.

In his junior year of 2009, Griffen recorded eight sacks, the fifth-best total in the conference. He was recognized as a second team All-Pac-10 for his efforts. Following USC's season-ending, 24-13, Emerald Bowl victory over Boston College, Griffen announced his intention to enter the 2010 NFL Draft, foregoing his final year of eligibility. That April, the Minnesota Vikings selected him in the fourth round.

Did You Know...?

Griffen attended the same high school as Hall of Fame player Randall McDaniel, whom he idolized as a young player. McDaniel played twelve years for Minnesota, coincidentally the same team that drafted Griffen.

A dominant force on the Vikings' offensive line, McDaniel was named to the first of 12 consecutive Pro Bowls starting in 1989, his sophomore year. Blocking for quarterbacks such as Rich Gannon, Warren Moon, and Randall Cunningham, McDaniel established himself as arguably the greatest guard in the history of the franchise.

Quarterback protection was integral to the team's success in 1998 as the Vikings had a near-perfect 15-1 season. The powerhouse offence led by Cunningham racked up a league-high 556 points. Minnesota looked poised to advance to Super Bowl XXXIII but was upset by the Atlanta Falcons in the NFC championship game. Kicker Gary Anderson, who hadn't missed an extra point or field goal all year, failed to convert a three-pointer that would have put the game out of reach late in the fourth quarter. Instead, Atlanta came back to tie the game, then won, 30-27, in overtime.

McDaniel played the final two years of his career in Tampa Bay, retiring at the end of the 2001 season. Between 1989 and 2001 he played in 202 consecutive games. He was named to the NFL's all-decade team of the 1990s and was enshrined into the Pro Football Hall of Fame in 2009.

Griffen appeared in Minnesota's final eleven games of 2010, having been inactive to start the year. The Vikings' fortunes went into a tailspin that season, and the team fired coach Brad Childress in November. Minnesota finished out of the playoffs after coming within a field goal of advancing to the Super Bowl the previous season.

THE CRIME...

Within a three-day period to close out January 2011, Griffen had two tumultuous run-ins with the law. On January 28, he was arrested for public intoxication following a Friday night on the town in Hollywood. He was released the next morning.

Then, on the afternoon of January 31, Griffen failed a routine traffic stop while driving in Los Angeles in a new Porsche. He was asked to produce his license, which turned out to be invalid. With the unfortunate weekend incident still fresh in his mind, Griffen told police he, "did not want to go back to jail" as reported by the *Los Angeles Times*. He then attempted to sprint from the scene. An officer gave chase and eventually caught up to Griffen, who responded by grabbing his pursuer in the crotch. Backup officers arrived and subdued Griffen with a taser.

The Vikings player was booked on suspicion of felony battery. He was released after posting a $50,000 bail.

WHAT FOLLOWED...

The next day, the district attorney's office in Los Angeles County declined to pursue felony charges, citing Griffen's absence of a criminal record and noting that the officer who was attacked was not injured in the altercation. The charges were downgraded to a misdemenaour. Griffen paid a $10,000 fine and was placed on probation.

Vikings coach Leslie Frazier and members of the team's front office insisted

"The mistakes I made, I was young, really didn't know right from wrong. Everything happens for a reason."

that Griffen sell his Porsche. They also enrolled the player into conditioning and development programs. It was a seminal turning point for Griffen, who decided to abandon his wayward lifestyle going forward.

Griffen has since matured and become a stalwart of the Vikings' defence. His 2012 season saw him register eight sacks and also return a 29-yard interception for a touchdown in a game against St. Louis. That October, Griffen endured personal tragedy with the sudden death of his mother, Sabrina Scott, after a spontaneous coronary artery dissection. She was just 52 years old. Despite the devastating circumstances, Griffen did not miss any games.

In March 2014, the Vikings signed Griffen to a five-year, $42.5 million contract, eliminating the risk of losing his services to free agency.

Reflecting on the regrettable weekend of 2011, Griffen spoke to the *St. Paul Pioneer Press* about changing his then-reckless ways. "The mistakes I made, I was young, really didn't know right from wrong. Everything happens for a reason," he said. "I'm blessed to be here now and show the Vikings my growth. I took it to the next level. Just hone in on that opportunity to be in the NFL."

MIKE VRABEL

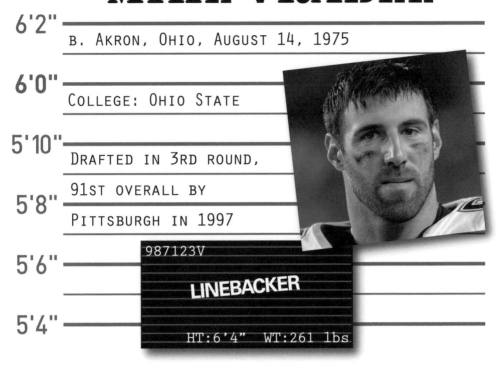

6'2"

b. Akron, Ohio, August 14, 1975

6'0"

College: Ohio State

5'10"

Drafted in 3rd round,

91st overall by

5'8"

Pittsburgh in 1997

987123V

5'6"

LINEBACKER

5'4"

HT:6'4"   WT:261 lbs

IN THE BEGINNING...

Mike Vrabel was a multi-sport athlete at Walsh Jesuit High School in Cayuhoga Falls, Ohio, excelling in football, basketball, and shot put. Using his size to full advantage, he registered 86 tackles and 12 sacks in his senior year on the way to becoming the district player of the year as selected by the *Akron Beacon Journal*. He was also named to the *USA Today* All-American second team.

From there, Ohio State University came calling, and Vrabel embarked on a collegiate career with the Buckeyes that was nothing short of legendary. He set school career records with 36 sacks and 66 tackles for loss during his tenure from 1993 to 1996. In his junior and senior years, Vrabel was named the Big Ten defensive player of the year. He graduated from OSU on a high note, earning consensus All-America honours while the number two ranked Buckeyes defeated Arizona State, 20-17, in the 1996 Rose Bowl.

Four months later, Vrabel was taken by the Pittsburgh Steelers in the fourth round of the 1997 NFL Draft. Coming out of training camp, he was one of eight rookies to make the final 53-man roster. Vrabel appeared in all but one of the team's games in the regular season, and Pittsburgh finished with a strong 11-5 record. The Steelers advanced to the AFC championship game where they were defeated by the Denver Broncos, the eventual Super Bowl champions.

Vrabel didn't reach the Super Bowl until he joined the New England Patriots. He had actually contemplated retirement but instead signed on with coach Bill

Did You Know…?

Besides his arrest and retirement, Vrabel made the headlines for a third, and very different, reason. He was one of ten players who filed an antitrust suit against the NFL in March in an attempt to prevent a lockout. Pro Bowl quarterbacks Tom Brady – Vrabel's Patriots teammate – Drew Brees and Peyton Manning were the biggest names seeking an eleventh-hour injunction prior to the expiration of the league's collective bargaining agreement.

The other players included Vincent Jackson, Ben Leber, Logan Mankins, Brian Robison, Osi Umenyiora, and college player Von Miller of Texas A&M.

At the heart of the labour dispute was the disagreement on how the owners and players should divide the NFL's $9.3 billion in annual revenues. Other issues on the table included the possibility of increasing the regular-season schedule from 16 to 18 games, and determining the level of players' access to owners' financial information.

After a seven-day extension of the CBA, the NFL locked out its players on March 12, 2011. One month later, Judge Susan Nelson forced the two sides in the players' anti-trust lawsuit to enter into mediation. The same judge ruled in favour of the players, lifting the lockout. But, a court of appeals granted a permanent stay of Judge Nelson's injunction, stalling mediation talks.

The NFL cancelled its May rookie symposium. The two sides negotiated into the summer. Finally, a new collective bargaining agreement was reached on July 25. Thus, amidst much fear and speculation of a shortened season, the league resolved its labour issues without a single game being cancelled.

Belichick's squad as a free agent in 2001. In Week 2, starting quarterback Drew Bledsoe suffered an injury after a devastating hit from New York Jets defensive end Mo Lewis. Tom Brady came on to replace Bledsoe, setting the stage for one of the most memorable stories in football. With Brady at the helm, the Patriots forged a mini-dynasty, winning three of the next four Super Bowls. Vrabel was instrumental in each victory, including a touchdown reception in Super Bowl XXXVIII.

In 2007, Vrabel earned the only Pro Bowl nomination of his career. The Patriots finished with a perfect 16-0 regular season but lost Super Bowl XLII to the New York Giants. After eight seasons in New England, Vrabel was traded, with quarterback Matt Cassell, to Kansas City for a second-round draft pick.

THE CRIME...

On April 4, 2011, Vrabel was arrested following an incident at the Belterra Casino Resort & Spa in Florence, Indiana. He was charged with a low-level felony theft after a casino employee spotted him taking bottles of alcohol from a deli without paying for them. Vrabel posted a $600 bond and was released shortly thereafter. The charge, upon conviction, carried a maximum penalty of six months to three years in jail, plus a maximum $10,000 fine.

"It was an unfortunate misunderstanding, and I take full responsibility for the miscommunication," Vrabel said in a statement through his agent. "I feel comfortable that after talking with the appropriate parties, we will resolve this matter."

It was the second run-in with the law for Vrabel. As a college player, he and a teammate had been arrested for assaulting a man in a parking lot. The offenders pleaded guilty to a lesser charge of disorderly conduct and were sentenced to 30 hours of community service.

Under the terms, the charges would be dropped if he wasn't charged with another crime for 180 days.

WHAT FOLLOWED…

In June, Vrabel entered into a diversion agreement. Under the terms, the charges would be dropped if he wasn't charged with another crime for 180 days.

The following month, Vrabel announced his retirement. Upon leaving the game, he had 57 career sacks to his credit, ranking him in the top-120 on the NFL's all-time list. "I am especially grateful to Bill Belichick and (Kansas City general manager) Scott Pioli, who not only gave me the opportunity to play for a team that won three Super Bowl championships and an NFL record 21 games in a row but also taught me invaluable lessons on creating the ultimate team approach," he said in a statement.

Vrabel immediately signed on with his alma mater, Ohio State, as the team's linebackers coach. He held the post for a year before switching roles, becoming the Buckeyes' defensive line coach.

In January 2014, Vrabel announced he was becoming the linebackers coach of the NFL's Houston Texans.

ALBERT HAYNESWORTH

6'2"

B. HARTSVILLE, SOUTH CAROLINA, JUNE 17, 1981

6'0"

COLLEGE: TENNESSEE

5'10"

DRAFTED IN 1ST ROUND,

15TH OVERALL BY

5'8"

TENNESSEE IN 2002

5'6"

366326H

DEFENSIVE TACKLE

5'4"

HT:6'6" WT:320 lbs

IN THE BEGINNING…

A ferocious tackler, Albert Haynesworth was ranked one of the top 100 high school players in the nation by ESPN.com during his senior year in which he recorded 110 tackles and six sacks. Although he was also a shot putter at Hartsville High School in his hometown, football was his forte, and he was named a SuperPrep All-American.

When the University of Tennessee beckoned, Haynesworth made an immediate impact, earning honours as a freshman All-American by *The Sporting News* in 1999. He and teammate John Henderson formed an impenetrable duo on the defensive line. In 2001, the Volunteers appeared headed to the Rose Bowl, but a disappointing loss to Louisiana State relegated them to the Citrus Bowl. Tennessee defeated the Michigan Wolverines, 45-17, in that matchup, Haynesworth's last college game.

It was a relatively short move from Knoxville to Nashville when Haynesworth was taken by the Tennessee Titans in the first round of the 2002 NFL Draft. He appeared in every game during his rookie pro season. The team won the AFC South Division and went all the way to the conference championship before losing to the Oakland Raiders. The next year, in what would be the first of many incidents displaying Haynesworth's volatility and instability, he kicked teammate Justin Hartwig in the chest.

In 2006, Haynesworth infamously received a five-game suspension from the NFL for kicking a helmetless opponent – centre Andre Gurode – in the face during a game against the Dallas Cowboys. The following season, he was fined $5,000 after slamming Jacksonville running back Maurice Jones-Drew to the ground following a tackle.

Haynesworth was a two-time Pro Bowler (2007 and 2008) and one of the league's most dominant defensive players when the Washington Redskins signed him to a lucrative, jaw-dropping, $100 million, seven-year contract as a free agent. But he clashed with coach Mike Shanahan publicly, skipped off-season workouts, and was a shadow of his former self on the field. In December 2010, he was suspended for the remainder of the season for conduct detrimental to the team. The signing turned out to be arguably the greatest bust in the history of NFL free agency.

THE CRIME...

In February 2011, Haynesworth was involved in two incidents. On February 12, he was charged with misdemeanour assault after a road rage altercation that had occurred ten days earlier. According to police reports, a 38-year-old driver, Arthur J. Velasquez, was punched by Haynesworth, who was tailgating him. The charge was dismissed when Velasquez, who suffered a bloody nose, reached an out-of-court settlement with Haynesworth.

A far more serious charge against Haynesworth was levied as a result of an allegation of sexual assault. A hotel waitress reported to police that, around 1:30am on February 13, she was clearing a table with her hands full. Haynesworth offered his credit card to the server. When the waitress nodded, the player slid the card down the front of her dress and groped her breast.

Haynesworth was officially charged with misdemeanour sexual abuse on April 26. The crime carried a maximum penalty of six months in jail and a fine of $1,000. The player's lawyer, A. Scott Bolden, maintained his client's innocence, saying that the charge was regretful and that witnesses would corroborate Haynesworth's story.

"Lazy, lack of passion and, a lot of times, a lack of character. And (Haynesworth) fits all three."

WHAT FOLLOWED...

The Redskins relieved themselves of their multi-million dollar headache in 2011 by trading Haynesworth to New England for a fifth-round draft pick.

That August, Haynesworth accepted a plea arrangement in which he agreed to undergo assessments for both alcohol abuse and psychological-social profiling. Under the terms, he also agreed to perform community service and to stay away from the waitress, whom he admitted to fondling. The charge was downgraded to simple assault, to which Haynesworth pleaded no contest.

After six games with the Patriots in 2011, Haynesworth was placed on waivers by the team following a sideline argument with defensive line coach Pepper Johnson. The player was claimed by Tampa Bay where he remained on the roster for the rest of the year. He was released by the Buccaneers in the off-season.

In February 2013, his conviction from the assault case was dismissed upon completion of more than 160 hours of community service. Bolden, Haynesworth's lawyer, said that his client was pleased to put the incident behind him and move on with his life.

Did You Know...?

The list of players and coaches who have verbally or physically sparred with Haynesworth appears endless.

In the last week of October 2013, the former Redskins player – two years removed from pro football – was still receiving jabs in the Washington media. Former teammate Chris Cooley called Haynesworth an awful human being who played only for the sake of collecting his exorbitant salary.

"His goal from the get-go was to take that money," Cooley told WTEM-AM radio. "He also indicated to many players on the team that his new goal was to get released as soon as possible. This was open (knowledge) among many players in this locker room: that his goal was basically to take money."

That same week, Haynesworth had appeared on Tennessee radio, calling coach Mike Shanahan "conniving" and predicting that the sideline boss would run Washington star quarterback Robert Griffin III into the ground. Shanahan had been vilified for leaving Griffin in the game too long in a wild card playoff loss to Seattle the previous season. Griffin suffered a devastating knee injury late in the game.

Addressing the Washington media in response, Shanahan retaliated in kind. "Let me put it this way: The only people I haven't gotten along with since I've been a coach – a head coach, an assistant coach – is someone that's lazy," Shanahan said at the podium. "Lazy, lack of passion and, a lot of times, a lack of character. And (Haynesworth) fits all three."

After leading the Redskins to the playoffs in 2012 – the team's first post-season appearance in five years – Shanahan was fired at the end of the 2013 season following a dreadful year in which the team won just three games.

SAM HURD

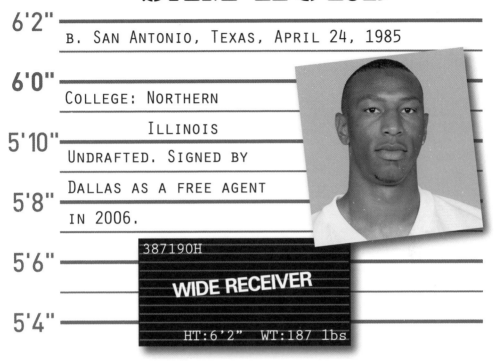

6'2"

B. SAN ANTONIO, TEXAS, APRIL 24, 1985

6'0"

COLLEGE: NORTHERN

ILLINOIS

5'10"

UNDRAFTED. SIGNED BY

DALLAS AS A FREE AGENT

5'8"

IN 2006.

387190H

5'6"

WIDE RECEIVER

5'4"

HT:6'2" WT:187 lbs

IN THE BEGINNING...

Sam Hurd grew up on the east side of San Antonio, the city's roughest and most underprivileged area, rampant with gangs and drug dealers. Although he had tattoos on his biceps representing gang culture, he personified the exact opposite of his seedy neighbourhood's reputation. At Brackenridge High School, Hurd taught special needs students while also lettering in football, basketball, and track and field.

Hurd didn't garner the attention of many college scouts, but eventually Northern Illinois became interested in recruiting him. He had a four-year career with the Huskies, culminating with a phenomenal senior year in which he caught 65 passes for 1,074 yards and 13 touchdowns, ranking him in the top-seven in the mid-American conference in each category. Upon graduating, Hurd had career marks of 2,322 receiving yards and 21 touchdowns, ranking him third and fourth, respectively, on the school's all-time list.

But there was scant interest in Hurd at the 2006 NFL Draft. By the time the 255th and last selection was announced, Hurd still hadn't heard his name called. The Dallas Cowboys signed him to a $285,000 free-agent rookie contract. Hurd worked under the mentorship of star receiver Terrell Owens and became a special teams contributor. However, Hurd could never move up the Cowboys' wide receivers' depth chart. When the exceptional Dez Bryant was drafted by the team in 2010, the writing was on the wall for Hurd's exit.

Although Hurd played the 2010 season in Dallas, he was released by the team in the off-season. He signed with Chicago as a free agent, appearing in 12 of the team's first 13 games of the year. When he stepped off the turf at Sports Authority Field at Mile High after a Bears overtime loss to the Denver Broncos, it would be for the final time.

Did You Know...?

In Week 5 of the 2006 season, Sam Hurd caught the first ever pass by Dallas Cowboys quarterback Tony Romo. Coming in relief of starter Drew Bledsoe in the third quarter, Romo found Hurd for a 33-yard strike. Dallas went on to beat the Houston Texans, 34-6.

Romo has been the Cowboys' starter ever since, with lukewarm results. That same season, Dallas traveled to Seattle for an NFC wild card playoff game. The Cowboys appeared poised to take a late fourth-quarter lead with a 19-yard field goal attempt. It should have been an easy three points, but Romo fumbled the snap. He recovered his own miscue but failed on his attempt to run the ball into the end zone. The Seahawks won, 21-20.

Over the years, Romo has developed a reputation for outstanding play over the first three months of the NFL season, only to struggle in games played in December and January. From 2006 to 2013, Romo has won just one playoff game while losing three.

THE CRIME...

On December 14, 2011, Hurd was arrested on federal drug charges by undercover agents in a Chicago restaurant. He was accused of cocaine possession, with the intent to distribute 500 grams or more of the substance. The investigation into Hurd's activities had started five months earlier, while Hurd was still in Dallas.

In July, police received a confidential tip of a drug deal involving four kilograms of cocaine. When the potential buyer was apprehended with $88,000 in a canvas bag, the man gave police Hurd's name as the owner of the cash. During a police interview, Hurd admitted he withdrew the money, but a subsequent investigation found an inconsistency between his bank records and the amount on hand.

A month later, police matched Hurd's cell-phone records to four people in California who were being held for narcotics and weapons offences. Finally, the same informant who was the source of the July tip arranged the Chicago meeting at which Hurd was arrested. At the meeting, Hurd negotiated prices for the intent to buy, "five to ten kilograms of cocaine and 1,000 pounds of marijuana per week for distribution in the Chicago area," according to the police complaint.

The informant, an undercover agent, gave Hurd a kilogram of cocaine which the football player took to his car. Hurd was arrested on the spot.

"We are disappointed whenever these circumstances arise," said the Chicago Bears in a statement. "We will deal with them appropriately once we have all the information."

Hurd was released the club two days later.

"My life is a train wreck because of the bad decisions I made."

WHAT FOLLOWED...

Hurd was indicted in January. While awaiting trial, he returned home to San Antonio to be with his wife Stacee Green and their two-year-old daughter. They sold their house and stayed with Hurd's sister. "I'm a blessed man. I get to do more of my father's work," Hurd told the *Chicago Tribune* as he took various volunteering jobs.

But in the summer of 2012, he was arrested again for testing positive for marijuana while out on bond, and he was held in federal custody. Prosecutors alleged that Hurd was once again trying to buy drugs with his co-defendant, his cousin Jesse Tyrone Chavful.

In April 2013, just before his trial was scheduled to begin, Hurd pleaded guilty to one count of conspiring to possess and distribute marijuana and cocaine.

Hurd received a 15-year prison term for his role in the drug operation, five years more than the minimum standard required by federal law. In handing down the sentence, Judge Jorge Solis originally contemplated a 27-year sentence but reduced the time by nearly half while noting that Hurd was a first-time offender.

"For some reason, you chose to go another route and go down the drug trafficking route," Judge Solis said to Hurd. "You wanted to get into it in a big way. You didn't just start nickel-and-diming it." Chavful received eight years for his role in the drug operation.

Several members of Hurd's family were in attendance at the hearing, but none of the player's teammates from either the Bears or Cowboys were present. Marion Barber, Hurd's teammate for six years, intended to show up but missed his flight.

"My life is a train wreck because of the bad decisions I made," Hurd told the courtroom. "Everything I did was a result of my marijuana addiction. I was extremely stupid. I feel the pain I caused my wife, mother, father, sisters and brothers and my community."

RYAN LEAF

6'2" — b. Great Falls, Montana, May 15, 1976

6'0" — College: Washington State

5'10" — Drafted in 1st round,

5'8" — 2nd overall by
San Diego in 1998

5'6" — 245090L

QUARTERBACK

5'4" — HT:6'5"   WT:245 lbs

IN THE BEGINNING...

Few players in the history of football, arguably in all of pro sports, went from potential superstar to draft bust as quickly and dramatically as Ryan Leaf. After quarterbacking Charles M. Russell High School in his hometown of Great Falls to the Montana AA state championship, he went on to Washington State University to have a prolific career with the Cougars. The year 1997 was a record-setting one for Leaf, who set Pac-10 Conference benchmarks with 3,968 passing yards and 34 touchdowns in just twelve games.

With Leaf at the helm, WSU advanced to the Rose Bowl for the first time in 67 years. The Cougars dropped a heartbreaking, 21-16, decision to Michigan that was mired in controversy. Leaf attempted to spike the ball as time was about to expire in the fourth quarter, but officials ruled that the clock had run to zero seconds remaining before the Cougars could run another play.

In spite of the bitter end to the season, Leaf was named the Pac-10 offensive player of the year and finished third in the voting for the Heisman Trophy. Charles Woodson – Michigan's outstanding defensive back – was the winner, while second place went to Tennessee's All-American quarterback, Peyton Manning.

After Leaf elected to forego his final year of college eligibility to enter the 1998 draft, speculation was rampant as to whether he or Manning would be chosen first overall. The top pick went to Indianapolis which chose Manning. Leaf was taken in the number two slot by San Diego.

Leaf immediately became the Chargers' number-one quarterback and started his pro career with a pair of wins, the first rookie QB to accomplish the feat since John Elway did so with Denver, 15 years earlier. But just as it seemed that Leaf's

Did You Know...?

Although it seems incomprehensible in retrospect, the anticipated decision over whether Ryan Leaf or Peyton Manning would be the first-overall pick in 1998 was close enough that it was dissected by pundits, executives, and coaches alike, as draft day approached.

A poll taken by *Newsday* had Leaf as the favourite: "Manning may have the more recognizable name, but Leaf clearly is the preferred quarterback among league executives. Fourteen of the 20 (general managers) polled said they would draft Leaf over Manning, citing the Washington State quarterback's stronger arm, better mobility, and more promising long-term prospect as a franchise-calibre player."

Indianapolis, which held the coveted top selection, elected to choose Manning, who evolved into the franchise's cornerstone. From 1998 to 2010, Manning was selected to eleven Pro Bowl teams with the Colts, winning MVP honours four times (sharing the award with Tennessee's Steve McNair in 2003). Manning was the most valuable player in Super Bowl XLI, throwing for 258 yards and a touchdown as Indianapolis defeated Chicago, 29-17.

Luckily for Colts fans, president and general manager Bill Polian – one year into his job – didn't listen to the majority of opinions on that draft day in 1998.

stock was on the rise, it plummeted very quickly. He threw six interceptions in his next two games and soon lost his starting job to Craig Whelian.

After a disappointing 1998 season in which he threw for just two touchdowns, Leaf missed the entire 1999 campaign with a shoulder injury. He won just once the following year – suffering a significant wrist injury along the way – and was released by the Chargers in February 2001. Tampa Bay then signed Leaf but released him prior to the start of the season in September.

The Dallas Cowboys took a chance on the beleaguered quarterback, but Leaf played in just four games – starting in three of them, all losses. Dallas released Leaf in 2002, after which the player signed with Seattle. However just before the start of the Seahawks' training camp, Leaf retired at age 26.

THE CRIME…

Leaf's personality didn't endear him to fans, teammates, or the media. In his most infamous outburst, he yelled an expletive at a San Diego reporter, adding "Don't talk to me, all right? Just knock it off!" His volatility may have been symptomatic of his addiction to painkillers. While out of professional football, Leaf spent six weeks in a treatment centre in Vancouver in 2008 after recognizing that he had a problem. Two years later, he pleaded guilty to seven counts of obtaining a controlled substance by fraud and was given ten years' probation and a $20,000 fine.

The rock bottom period in Leaf's life came within a three-day stretch in the spring of 2012. On March 30, he was arrested after police said he broke into a friend's home and stole a bottle of prescription painkillers, specifically oxycodone pills. He was released on a $76,000 bond and charged with burglary, theft, and possession of a dangerous drug.

Then, on April Fools' Day, homeowners in Great Falls returned to their residence to find Leaf inside. The former player said he had the wrong house and left the premises, but not before taking three bottles of prescription medication. Leaf was arrested the next day after the homeowners alerted authorities.

Bond was set at $101,000, but Leaf could not be released because he had violated his probation.

Leaf was sentenced to five years in jail, nine months of which was to be spent in a drug-treatment facility instead of prison.

WHAT FOLLOWED...

In May, Leaf reached a bargain in which he pleaded guilty to charges of burglary and felony drug possession. In exchange, the prosecution dropped two burglary charges and one drug charge. Leaf was sentenced to five years in jail, nine months of which was to be spent in a drug-treatment facility instead of prison.

In acknowledging his family, Leaf expressed remorse for his actions. "They believe I've held them for ransom for 36 years, and I don't know why I should have to do that anymore," Leaf said, as reported in the *Great Falls Tribune*. "I'm lazy and dishonest and selfish. These were behaviours I had before my addiction kicked in."

Leaf was terminated from the treatment program in January 2013 and sent to prison after he threatened a staff member at the facility where he had been under supervision. The incident was one of several violations of the conditions of his program, according to a statement released by the Montana Department of Corrections.

CHAD JOHNSON

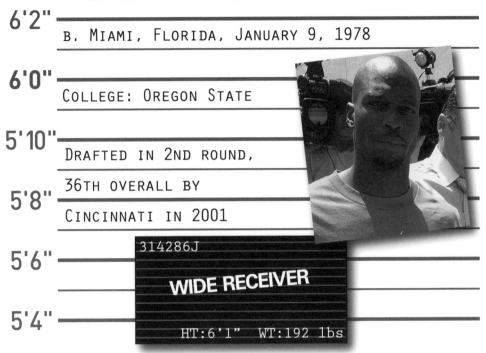

6'2"

B. MIAMI, FLORIDA, JANUARY 9, 1978

6'0"

COLLEGE: OREGON STATE

5'10"

DRAFTED IN 2ND ROUND,

36TH OVERALL BY

5'8"

CINCINNATI IN 2001

5'6"

314286J

WIDE RECEIVER

5'4"

HT:6'1" WT:192 lbs

IN THE BEGINNING...

Cocky and flamboyant, Chad Johnson was a polarizing figure throughout his eleven-year NFL career. His athleticism and talent won the hearts of many fans, especially in Cincinnati where he played all but one of his pro seasons. But his egocentric, boisterous attitude drew the wrath of opponents, critics, and even his own coaches.

Johnson played his senior college year of 2000 at Oregon State University under coach Dennis Erickson. He caught eight passes for touchdowns to lead the Pac-10 Conference in that category, while finishing second with an average of 21.8 yards per reception. Playing alongside future NFL teammate T.J. Houshmandzadeh, Johnson and the Beavers earned a trip to the Fiesta Bowl where they easily handled Notre Dame, 41-9, to finish the season with eleven wins against just one defeat.

The Cincinnati Bengals selected Johnson in the second round of the 2001 draft, using the receiver sparingly in his rookie season. Johnson appeared in twelve of the team's 16 games – three times as a starter – catching 28 passes for 329 yards and a touchdown. Two years later, Johnson had a breakout campaign, earning his first of five consecutive Pro Bowl selections in 2003. He was fourth in the NFL in both receiving yards (1,355) and receiving touchdowns (ten).

By 2005, Johnson was established as an All-Pro-calibre receiver. However, he earned Bengals coach Marvin Lewis's disapproval by hanging a sheet of paper in his locker listing his opposing cornerbacks, titled "Who Covered 85 in '05," 85 being his jersey number. Lewis replaced the list with one of his own that read, "Did 85 do everything he could to lead the team to victory?"

Johnson established a reputation for premeditated, over-exuberant touchdown celebrations. Once, after catching a pass in the end zone, he mimicked performing CPR on the football. In another instance, he bent down on one knee to simulate a marriage proposal to a Bengals cheerleader. Johnson's trash talking in the media was seen as flippant and arrogant.

In 2008, Johnson legally changed his last name to Ochocinco, the Spanish word for his number. He played in Cincinnati for three years before being traded to New England. With an abundance of talented personnel available to quarterback Tom Brady, notably Wes Welker and Rob Gronkowski, Ochocinco was used sparingly. The Patriots finished the season at 13-3, advancing to Super Bowl XLVI before losing to the New York Giants.

Ochocinco was released by the Patriots in June 2012, signing with Miami as a free agent days later.

THE CRIME...

Independence Day was a happy holiday for Ochocinco and his new wife, Evelyn Lozada, as they exchanged vows that afternoon. Three weeks later, the player changed his name back to Johnson. As Johnson walked off the field after playing in the Dolphins' pre-season game on August 10, he appeared to be blissfully looking forward to the start of a new season.

The next night, Johnson was arrested on domestic violence charges. According to the police report, Johnson and Lozada got into an argument that was precipitated by Lozada's discovering a shopping receipt for a box of condoms. Johnson grabbed Lozada and head-butted her on the forehead, causing a three-inch laceration.

Lozada fled to a neighbour's house for safety. Police arrived at the couple's home where they took Johnson into custody, despite his insistence that his wife initiated the head-butt. Lozada was treated in hospital for her injuries while Johnson was released after posting a $2,500 bond.

WHAT FOLLOWED...

Less than 24 hours after the arrest, the Dolphins released Johnson. "With any type of these decisions, it was not an easy one," coach Joe Philbin said in a news conference. "It was not reactive nor was it based on one single incident."

Lozada immediately filed for divorce, saying that the marriage was "irretrievably broken." In a statement, she said she was deeply disappointed that Johnson hadn't taken responsibility for his actions. The divorce was finalized on September 19.

"To all the fans and supporters I have disappointed, you have my sincerest apologies."

In his first statement since the arrest, Johnson expressed remorse to Lozada and to his fans. "I would like to wish Evelyn well and will never say anything bad about her because I truly love her to death. To all the fans and supporters I have disappointed, you have my sincerest apologies," he said.

Johnson pleaded no contest to misdemeanour domestic battery in an agreement that spared him jail time. He was placed on probation and agreed to have no contact with Lozada.

In June 2013, Johnson appeared in a courtroom after failing to keep in touch with his probation officer. His lawyer, Adam Swickle, arranged a plea deal to keep him out of jail for the violation. The agreement was initially accepted by Judge Kahtleen McHugh, but after Johnson gave Swickle a congratulatory, appreciative slap on the butt, McHugh admonished Johnson for not appearing to take the hearing seriously. She then rejected the bargain, and sentenced the former player to 30 days in custody. Johnson served seven days before being released after apologizing to McHugh.

Did You Know…?

Johnson's ex-wife, Evelyn Lozada, has made headlines for becoming romantically involved with star athletes. Before marrying Johnson (then known as Ochocinco), Lozada – a regular member of VH1's Basketball Wives – had once been engaged to NBA power forward Antoine Walker.

In December 2013, Lozada announced her engagement to Los Angeles Dodgers outfielder Carl Crawford. A veteran who spent most of his Major League Baseball career with Tampa Bay before moving to Boston and later L.A., Crawford is a four-time All-Star and has led the American League in stolen bases four times. He won an American League Silver Slugger Award in 2010.

Lozada and Crawford welcomed a baby boy – Carl Leo Crawford – in March 2014. He is the first child of Crawford, while Lozada has an adult daughter from a previous relationship that she had in her teens, well before she started "playing the field" of professional sports.

JOSH BRENT

6'2"   B. BLOOMINGTON, ILLINOIS, JANUARY 30, 1988

6'0"   COLLEGE: ILLINOIS

5'10"   DRAFTED IN 7TH ROUND OF

5'8"   SUPPLEMENTAL DRAFT BY

   DALLAS IN 2010

009486B

DEFENSIVE TACKLE

HT:6'2" WT:321 lbs.

5'6"

5'4"

IN THE BEGINNING...

Attending Central Catholic High School in his hometown of Bloomington, Illinois, Josh Brent used his size and strength to develop a remarkable athletic career. The state champion at shot put in his junior season, Brent was also a defensive standout on the school's football team, recording 109 tackles and six sacks. He earned several recognitions in his senior year, including All-American honours from both PrepStar and SuperPrep. While recruiters from universities Ohio State, Michigan, and Wisconsin had their eyes on Brent, the player chose to remain in his home state to play for Illinois.

In his freshman year of 2007, Brent appeared in all but two of his team's games as the Illini finished with a record of 9-4 to become the 20th-ranked team in the nation. In its final game of the season, Illinois was pummeled, 49-17, by Southern California in the Rose Bowl.

Over the next two years, Brent earned more starts, forcing three fumbles in 2009 to become one of the Big Ten conference leaders in that statistic. The player was academically ineligible to play in his senior college year. As a result, the Dallas Cowboys used the NFL Supplemental Draft to select him in 2010.

Brent made the team's 53-man roster. Despite playing backup tackle to Pro Bowl star Jay Ratliff, Brent played in all 16 of the Cowboys' games during his first professional year, recording 14 solo tackles. He had a setback in 2011, missing all of December with a knee injury and making just six appearances on the season.

In 2012, Brent appeared to be back on track, taking advantage of more time on the field as a result of injuries to Ratliff. Brent played in all of Dallas's first twelve games, making a total of five tackles in the last two appearances of that stretch. But on the day before the team's game against Cincinnati on December 9, his life was irrevocably altered.

Did You Know...?

Jerry Brown's mother Stacey Jackson has shown resilient strength and courage in the wake of the tragedy. Right up to the end of Josh Brent's trial, she and Brent had spoken every week since the crash which claimed the life of her son.

"If being mad at Josh would bring Jerry back, I would be the No. 1 person. I would be mad as hell at him," Jackson told the *Dallas Morning News*. "It takes too much time and too much energy to be mad and frustrated at him when who is me? I'm a nobody."

Brown's first child, a daughter named Mya Lee Brown, was born seven weeks after the accident. Jackson maintains contact with both the baby's mother, Andrea Bosquez, and her granddaughter.

In addition, Jackson has forged a strong bond with Dallas owner Jerry Jones and coach Jason Garrett. Each of the two men phones Brown's mother at least every other month to check in on her.

"For them to call and do that is special. The Dallas Cowboys are in a class by themselves," Jackson said.

THE CRIME...

At around 2:20am, just before the Cowboys players were scheduled to fly out of Dallas for their game in Cincinnati, Brent was driving his Mercedes with his best friend Jerry Brown as a passenger. The two players were not only teammates with the Cowboys, but they had played together for three years at Illinois. The speeding vehicle was heading west on the service road of State Highway 114 when it flipped after hitting a curb. The overturned car slid on its roof for almost 900 feet. Neither man was wearing a seat belt.

Brent dragged Brown from the car, which was on fire. While officers attended to the small blaze, paramedics found Brown unresponsive at the scene. Brown, at age 25, was pronounced dead at the hospital.

Brent failed a sobriety test and was promptly arrested on suspicion of drunk driving. It was his second such incident. He had been booked for DUI and driving without a license while a college junior at Illinois, three years earlier, serving half of a 60-day jail sentence as a result.

An inconsolable Brent released a statement via his agent. "I am devastated and filled with grief, filled with grief for the loss of my close friend and teammate, Jerry Brown," Brent said. "I am also grief-stricken for his family, friends, and all who were blessed enough to have known him. I will live with this horrific and tragic loss every day for the rest of my life. My prayers are with his family, our teammates, and his friends at this time."

"I am devastated and filled with grief, filled with grief for the loss of my close friend and teammate, Jerry Brown."

The next day, the Cowboys took to the field at Paul Brown Stadium against the Cincinnati Bengals with heavy hearts. Dallas kicker Dan Bailey booted a 40-yard field goal on the final play of the game to seal a 20-19 win for the mourning Cowboys.

WHAT FOLLOWED...

While out on bond, Brent was returned to jail in June 2013 after twice testing positive for marijuana. Nevertheless, the Cowboys kept him on their roster. With an NFL suspension looming, Brent instead opted to retire from the NFL on July 18. His trial was postponed until the following January.

When legal proceedings finally got underway, testimony was provided indicating that Brent had been going 110 miles per hour in a 45 mph zone when the crash occurred. His blood alcohol level was 0.18, more than twice the legal limit in Texas.

One of Brent's lawyers argued that his client didn't have as much to drink as prosecutors had contended and alleged that the blood alcohol tests administered by police were inaccurate.

Prosecutors, pressing for jail time, countered by pointing to Brent's 2009 DUI arrest.

Brent was sentenced to 180 days in jail and given 10 years' probation. He had faced as much as 20 years in prison. At the time of his incarceration, the Cowboys still held his professional rights.

Jerry Brown's mother Stacey Jackson, stated her forgiveness for Brent: "He's still responsible, but you can't go on in life holding a grudge. We all make mistakes," said Jackson, as reported by the *Associated Press*.

ANDRE SMITH

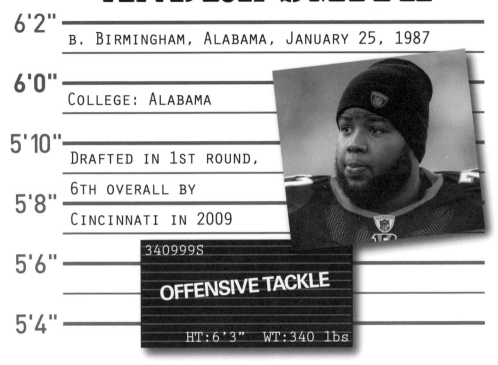

6'2" B. BIRMINGHAM, ALABAMA, JANUARY 25, 1987

6'0" COLLEGE: ALABAMA

5'10" DRAFTED IN 1ST ROUND,

5'8" 6TH OVERALL BY
CINCINNATI IN 2009

340999S

5'6"

OFFENSIVE TACKLE

5'4"

HT:6'3" WT:340 lbs

IN THE BEGINNING...

Opposing pass rushers trying to get at Huffman High School's quarterbacks were likely stifled by Andre Smith, an imposing figure on the offensive line of the Birmingham, Alabama school's football team. Named Alabama's Mr. Football by the state's sportswriters' association, Smith was one of four finalists for the Walter Payton Trophy, given to the best high school player in the United States in that sport.

Smith chose to attend university in his home state, suiting up on the gridiron for the Alabama Crimson Tide. In his first two seasons beginning in 2006, Smith started in all of his team's games. His junior season of 2008 was his finest as Smith, a Consensus All-American, won the John Outland Trophy for being the best interior lineman in the NCAA. The Tide rolled to a 12-2 record and were ranked the sixth-best team in the nation.

In a 2009 draft rife with talent, Smith was taken by Cincinnati in the first round ahead of players such as Michael Crabtree, Clay Matthews, and Percy Harvin. But contract negotiations between the player and the Bengals organization lasted well into August and Smith missed three of team's four pre-season games. An episode of the HBO show "Hard Knocks" featured teammates mocking Smith's 340-pound girth. Finally both sides came to terms on a four-year deal worth $21 million, with a club option to make it a six-year deal at $29.5 million. Just when Smith appeared to be embarking on his pro career, his plans were derailed by a foot injury suffered at the end of training camp.

Injuries limited Smith to just 13 games over his first two seasons. In 2011, Smith finally became a regular starter, providing security for quarterback Andy Dalton while clearing lanes for running back Cedric Benson, who rushed for over 1,000 yards. The next year, Smith played in all 17 regular season and playoff games and was named a first team All-NFL player by the website Pro Football Focus. The Bengals finished 10-6 in the regular season, losing a wild card post-season game to the Houston Texans.

THE CRIME...

Smith was arrested on January 18, 2013, at Atlanta's Hartsfield Jackson International Airport after officials at a security checkpoint discovered a .38-calibre handgun in his carry-on luggage. After being charged with carrying a weapon in an unauthorized location, Smith was released from jail upon posting a $3,000 bond.

The incident was the seventh firearms-related arrest of an NFL player within a three-year period and occurred at a time when the NFL was still recovering from a gun-related tragedy. Seven weeks earlier, on December 1, 2012, Kansas City linebacker Jovan Belcher fatally shot his girlfriend, then drove himself to the Chiefs' facility before turning the gun on himself in front of horrified coaches and staff.

Belcher's former Chiefs teammate Thomas Jones defended the need for players

Did You Know...?

The Alabama Crimson Tide was forced to nullify 21 football wins between 2005 and 2007, the latter two years marking the beginning of Andre Smith's college career. The sanctions were imposed in June 2009 as a result of the school's involvement in improperly obtaining free textbooks. Altogether, 16 of the university's athletics teams were put on three years' probation. The school was also fined $43,900.

A total of 201 student athletes were cited for obtaining the free books, including football players Antoine Caldwell, Marlon Davis, Glen Coffee, Chris Rodgers, and Marquis Johnson. The football players were suspended four games each after the violations were uncovered midway through the 2007 season. By that time, Alabama had posted a record of 5-2 under new head coach Nick Saban.

Under NCAA rules, athletes were declared ineligible from the time they received the improper benefits. Seven football players were identified by the NCAA for the infraction. The governing body asked Alabama to identify the games in which those players competed. The list of such games included 21 Alabama victories, which were erased from the record books.

As a result, the Tide's 2005 record of 10-2 was adjusted to 0-2 by the NCAA, while their 2006 mark of 6-7 was adjusted to 0-7. All but one of the games played within that span was coached by Mike Shula, who was fired in November 2006.

The team's 7-6 mark in 2007 was adjusted to 2-6. The team received credit for its victories against Tennessee and versus Colorado in the Independence Bowl.

to carry guns. "Most guys when they first come into the league is when they first start to realize they need protection," Jones told *USA Today*. "People will go to any length to take what you have or harm you in some way just because they don't have what you have. If you don't have a firearm to protect you from situations, and God forbid something happens to you, you wish you would have a firearm."

The NFL's guns and weapons policy prohibits the possession of a firearm by any player while performing any service for the team or the league, or while on the premises of any NFL stadium or facility.

WHAT FOLLOWED…

Coach Marvin Lewis responded by saying of Smith: "He's a smart guy that got involved in a dumb situation that caused him an embarrassment for a moment," as reported by the *Cincinnati Enquirer*.

Three months after the arrest, on April 18, Smith, through his Twitter account @BigSmitty71, announced, "Great relief and excitement of the resolve of my issue in January. Moving Ahead Fast Forward. I am grateful." One week later, the Bengals signed Smith – an unrestricted free agent – to a three-year, $18 million contract.

Smith missed a mandatory mini-camp in June due to personal reasons and was fined by the team. Nevertheless, he appeared in all of the Bengals' games during the 2013 season. Cincinnati won eleven games en route to finishing first in the AFC North Division, but the team was ousted in the wild card round of the playoffs by San Diego.

"People will go to any length to take what you have or harm you in some way just because they don't have what you have."

AUSAR WALCOTT

6'2"

B. HACKENSACK, NEW JERSEY, JANUARY 7, 1990

6'0"

COLLEGE: VIRGINIA

5'10"

UNDRAFTED. SIGNED AS A

FREE AGENT BY CLEVELAND

5'8"

IN 2013.

5'6"

314286W

DEFENSIVE END

5'4"

HT:6'4" WT:240 lbs

IN THE BEGINNING...

Ausar Walcott was a versatile athlete at Hackensack High School in his hometown. He earned all-county honours as a sprinter and long jumper while playing both offensive and defensive positions on the football team. His forte was preventing points rather than scoring them. Walcott made 80 tackles in his senior year and was a highly-ranked prospect by the website Rivals and Scout by the time he was ready to graduate.

Walcott chose to attend the University of Virginia, where he was a redshirted freshman in 2008. The next year, he earned his first letter for the Cavaliers, appearing in ten of the team's 12 games, all on special teams. In his sophomore season, Walcott made the move from safety to linebacker. A run-in with the law occurred in February 2011 when Walcott and two teammates were arrested after a fight near the campus of James Madison University. Assault charges against

Walcott – who was briefly suspended for conduct detrimental to the team – were later dismissed.

Walcott made one more transition during his college career, shifting to defensive end prior to the start of his 2012 senior season. Walcott's first game starting at his new position came against Georgia Tech. He was credited with 30 tackles in his final college year.

In four years at Virginia, Walcott recorded 50 solo tackles while assisting on 78 others. After he was passed over at the 2013 NFL Draft, he elected to try out with the Cleveland Browns. The team signed him to a three-year, $1.5 million free agent contract on May 13.

THE CRIME…

On June 23, 2013, Walcott reportedly punched a man in the head outside the Palace Gentleman's Club, a Passaic, New Jersey establishment. The altercation between Alcott and 24-year-old Derrick Jones occurred at around 3am, according to police reports. Jones was taken to hospital in critical condition.

Jones's aunt phoned police to report the assault. After conducting an investigation, detectives identified Walcott as a suspect. Two days later, Walcott was

---

"Even though I didn't do anything, if I would have just walked away, I never would have even been in this situation and everything would have been cleared."

---

arrested after he turned himself in to the authorities. He was charged with first-degree attempted murder, second-degree aggravated assault, and third-degree endangering an injured victim, facing as many as ten to 20 years in prison. Bail was set at $500,000.

Walcott's coach at Hackensack High School, Gordon Whiting, told *The Record* (Bergen County, New Jersey) that he was stunned by the news of the arrest. "He is a great kid, a hard-working kid. He was never a discipline problem," Whiting said.

The next day, the Browns cut Walcott from their roster.

 WHAT FOLLOWED...

Jones was discharged from hospital and was sent to a rehabilitation centre to recover from a brain injury. While Walcott remained in custody, his coaches, high-school classmates, and even Hackensack's police commissioner wrote letters in support of their local alumnus. A New Jersey state judge was persuaded to reduce Walcott's bail to $85,000. After the sum was posted, he was released.

NFL Commissioner Roger Goodell blocked any team from signing Walcott as a free agent. In daily transaction reports sent to all thirty-two teams, Goodell stated that he would not approve of any signing until he, "conducts a hearing and determines any appropriate discipline under the Personal Conduct Policy."

In October 2013, a grand injury indicted Walcott on the less serious charges of aggravated assault and endangering an injured victim but dropped the attempted murder count. While awaiting trial on the reduced charges, which carried a maximum ten-year sentence, Walcott – through his defence attorney Miles Feinstein – has maintained his innocence.

Prosecutors contend that, although only one punch was thrown in the incident, the strike came without any provocation from Jones. Feinstein has countered that the act came in self-defence after a large group of people was moving towards his client, who was retreating.

Walcott rejected a plea deal in February 2014 that would have required him to serve a seven-year sentence. Under the terms, he would have had to plead guilty to second-degree aggravated assault and serve at least 85 per cent of his time before becoming parole eligible.

As of spring 2014, Walcott is still awaiting trial, and also a decision from Goodell regarding his NFL playing status.

Did You Know...?

The 2011 incident at James Madison University occurred as a result of Ausar Walcott and two Virginia teammates – Devin Wallace and Mike Price – entering an apartment complex near the campus and assaulting three male victims, two of whom required hospital treatment for non-life-threatening injuries.

A verbal altercation outside a party had ensued on January 30, just after 1:30am, when the football players accused their victims of directing racial slurs towards them (Walcott and Wallace are both black). The confrontation escalated after the players entered the apartment where the party was being hosted.

After warrants were issued for their arrests, each player turned himself in to police. All three Cavaliers faced misdemeanour charges of assault and battery by mob, and one felony charge of burglary-entering a dwelling with intent to commit assault. They were suspended indefinitely by the team by Virginia coach Mike London.

Walcott was reinstated after he underwent sessions with the team's sports psychologist, Jim Bauman. Those who also counseled him included his mother, Pamela Robinson, the team's football chaplain, George Morris, and special teams coordinator, Anthony Poindexter.

Reflecting on his brief suspension in the incident, Alcott told the *Washington Post*, "I spent a lot of that time [when he was suspended] by myself, getting help on things that I can do to improve on myself and make myself a better person, as well as a better player."

All charges against Walcott were dropped, but the player recognized the error of his ways. "My gut kind of did tell me to walk away, and I should have," Walcott said. "Even though I didn't do anything, if I would have just walked away, I never would have even been in this situation and everything would have been cleared."

AARON HERNANDEZ

B. BRISTOL, CONNECTICUT, NOVEMBER 6, 1989

6'2"

6'0"

COLLEGE: FLORIDA

5'10"

DRAFTED IN 4TH ROUND,

113TH OVERALL BY NEW

5'8"

ENGLAND IN 2010

724101H

5'6"

TIGHT END

5'4"

HT:6'2" WT:250 lbs

IN THE BEGINNING…

From a young age, Aaron Hernandez was destined for football greatness. As a senior at Bristol Central High School in his Connecticut hometown, Hernandez was named both the state's Gatorade football player of the year, and *Hartford Courant* player of the year for the 2006-07 season. But through all the accolades, the athletic tight end was coping with the untimely passing of his father, Dennis.

The elder Hernandez succumbed to complications following routine hernia surgery in January 2006, at just 49 years of age. Grief-stricken, Aaron Hernandez rebelled against his teachers, coaches, and his widowed mother. Enrolling at the University of Florida, the player honoured his late father with a tattoo that read "If it is to be, it is up to me," a favourite saying of his dad's.

In 2008, Hernandez's sophomore season, the Gators rolled to a 12-1 record for a berth in the BCS championship game, led by defending Heisman Trophy-winning quarterback Tim Tebow. With the national championship on the line, Hernandez caught five passes for 57 yards, and Tebow threw for a pair of touchdowns as Florida defeated Oklahoma, 24-14.

One year later, Hernandez won the John Mackey Award, given to the best tight end in college football. He waived his final year of college eligibility to enter the 2010 NFL Draft. Teams were wary of selecting Hernandez, a player who had failed multiple drug tests for marijuana during his time at Florida. As a result, Hernandez wasn't taken until the fourth-round, by New England.

The gamble for the Patriots paid huge dividends. Hernandez and fellow rookie tight end Rob Gronkowski, along with wide receivers Wes Welker and Deion Branch, gave quarterback Tom Brady an arsenal of weapons at his disposal. New England marched to a 14-2 record in 2010, only to be upset by the New York Jets in the

Did You Know...?

Hernandez was touted to be a first-round selection 2010, but his involvement with marijuana was a red flag for many NFL executives. With the league's stringent substance-abuse policy in effect, Hernandez was a prime candidate for a possible suspension.

In a letter obtained by the *Boston Globe*, Hernandez wrote to Patriots executive Nick Caserio and agreed to bi-weekly drug tests if New England drafted him.

"In addition, I will tie any guaranteed portion of my 2010 compensation to these drug tests and reimburse the team a pro-rata amount for any failed drug test," Hernandez continued. "I ask you to trust me when I say you have absolutely nothing to worry about when it comes to me and the use of recreational drugs. I have set very high goals for myself in the NFL and am focused 100% on achieving those goals."

True to his word, Hernandez was never suspended for drug use or any other infraction during his three-year playing career.

But under the circumstances of his arrest and indictment, the player is currently under indefinite suspension by the NFL. With the prospect of facing life behind bars, the ban is a mere technicality.

divisional round of the playoffs. The next year, Hernandez caught passes for 910 yards as the undefeated Patriots advanced to Super Bowl XLVI, where they fell, 21-17, to the New York Giants.

In the summer 2012, the Patriots invested heavily in Hernandez and Gronkowski, signing both players to significant contract extensions. Hernandez's deal had a maximum value of $40 million. It included a signing bonus of $12.5 million, the largest ever for an NFL tight end. Hernandez was limited to ten games that season due to a high ankle sprain. He registered 483 receiving yards and five touchdowns in 2012.

Eight days after police first scoured Hernandez's home for evidence, the player was arrested and charged with first-degree murder in Lloyd's death.

THE CRIME...

Police obtained warrants to enter and search Hernandez's home in North Attleborough, Massachusetts, on June 18, 2013, as they investigated the shooting death of Odin Lloyd. The victim was dating the sister of Hernandez's girlfriend, Shayanna Jenkins. The day before, another group of officers had discovered Lloyd's body in an industrial park just a mile and a half from where Hernandez lived. The player aroused suspicion by turning over his cellphone – which had been destroyed – to investigators, while also summoning a team of house cleaners to his mansion on the day Lloyd's body was found.

Eight days after police first scoured Hernandez's home for evidence, the player was arrested and charged with first-degree murder in Lloyd's death. He was also charged with five weapons offences. Hernandez was led from his residence in handcuffs and taken in to custody.

The Patriots released him from their roster just two hours later. "A young man was murdered last week, and we extend our sympathies to the family and friends who mourn his loss," said the team in a press release. "Words cannot express the disappointment we feel knowing that one of our players was arrested as a result of this investigation."

In the ensuing 48 hours, two of Hernandez's alleged accomplices, Carlos Oritz and Ernest Wallace, were also arrested in connection with the grisly crime.

WHAT FOLLOWED...

On August 22, 2013, Hernandez was indicted by a grand jury for first-degree murder. He pleaded not guilty at his arraignment, two weeks later.

Prosecutors assembled a timeline of the events surrounding Lloyd's death as they constructed their case. They alleged that the player was angry with Lloyd for talking with a group of Hernandez's enemies at a night club, just days before the shooting. On the night of the murder, Hernandez, Ortiz, Wallace, and Lloyd drove in a Nissan Altima. Around 3:30am, Lloyd was shot three times in an execution-style manner with a .45 calibre Glock soon after he exited the vehicle. Two more bullets were fired into his chest as he lay on the ground.

Hernandez is being held without bail as he awaits trial. The Patriots have cut all ties with the player, whose release has resulted in the forfeiture of the remainder of his salary. The team removed all memorabilia, including jerseys bearing his name, from their pro shop shortly after the arrest. All companies with whom Hernandez had engaged in endorsement deals have terminated their respective sponsorships.

DARREN SHARPER

6'2"

B. RICHMOND, VIRGINIA, NOVEMBER 3, 1975

6'0"

COLLEGE: WILLIAM & MARY

5'10"

DRAFTED IN 2ND ROUND,

60TH OVERALL BY GREEN

5'8"

BAY IN 1997

442286S

5'6"

DEFENSIVE BACK / SAFETY

5'4"

HT:6'2" WT:210 lbs

IN THE BEGINNING...

Despite playing quarterback at Hermitage High School in Virginia, Darren Sharper made the move to defensive back at the urging of Jimmye Laylock, his coach at William & Mary University. Sharper's mentor obviously had a keen eye for maximizing his players' talent. Sharper was named a three-time All-American at the defensive position while setting a school record with 24 interceptions over his four-year career. In 1996, Sharper's senior season, he was named the Yankee Conference defensive player of the year.

The Green Bay Packers – the defending Super Bowl champions – chose Sharper in the second round of the 1997 draft. Although he didn't start in any of his team's games in his rookie campaign, Sharper opportunistically displayed his speed and skill coming off the bench for coach Mike Holmgren with a pair of interceptions for touchdowns. The Packers won the NFC championship, but their bid for a second consecutive championship was thwarted by the Denver Broncos.

Sharper became a full-time starter in 1998, entering into the Packers' secondary as a free safety. After three straight appearances in the conference championships, Green Bay bowed out to San Francisco in a wild card game. Holmgren resigned his post in the off-season to become the coach of the Seattle Seahawks.

Two years later, Sharper enjoyed a career season, leading the NFL with nine interceptions on the way to his first Pro Bowl selection, in 2000. Sharper delighted the 'cheeseheads' at Lambeau Field with a second Pro Bowl nod in 2002, registering 233 yards on interception returns, the best in the league in that category.

After eight seasons in Green Bay, Sharper signed with the Minnesota Vikings as a free agent. In his first year with the new club, Sharper matched a career season-best total with nine interceptions in 2005. The player continued to climb the NFL's all-time career interception list, notching his 50th and 51st career picks in a Week 2 game against Detroit.

In March 2009, Sharper ended his four-year tenure with Minnesota, signing as a free agent with the New Orleans Saints. Not only did Sharper earn his fifth career Pro Bowl selection that season, but he won his only career Super Bowl,

Did You Know...?

Sharper was fired from his job as a commentator on NFL Network in February 2014. He had been suspended without pay following his initial arrest the previous month, but the league – in its initiative to uphold a minimum standard of personal conduct – terminated Sharper's employment, despite the principle of presumption of innocence.

Conversely, NBC did not have to make such a decision in 1994, when then-broadcaster O.J. Simpson was arrested for double homicide. NBC Sports president Dick Ebersol told the *New York Times* three years later, "When I visited him in jail, he said he never planned to work again in the business."

Simpson was later acquitted of the double murder charges against him.

making three tackles in the championship game as the Saints defeated the Indianapolis Colts.

Injuries forced Sharper to miss half of the 2010 campaign, after which he retired, having played 14 seasons in the NFL. He was named to the Pro Football Hall of Fame's All-2000's second team, and he ranks tied for second with Charles Woodson on the league's all-time list for interception returns for touchdowns with eleven, one behind Rod Woodson as of 2013.

THE CRIME...

On January 17, 2014, Sharper was arrested in Los Angeles in connection with two sexual assaults that were reported to have occurred in the city's west end. His bail was set at $200,000.

Allegations surfaced that, on two occasions, Sharper invited two women to his hotel room, drugged them, and raped them. The first incident was reported to have occurred on October 30, 2013. As reported by the New Orleans *Times-Picayune*, prosecutors contend that Sharper gave both women a liquid shot, possibly containing Ambien and morphine, causing them to pass out. One of the women woke up with Sharper sexually assaulting her, according to her account provided to investigators.

Prosecutors say Sharper repeated the deed on January 14, meeting two different women at the same night club in West Hollywood where he met his alleged victims. As was the case three months earlier, the women were offered shots containing the date rape drugs, losing consciousness as a result. Upon awakening several hours later, they both sought medical treatment while one of the women phoned police, believing that she had been sexually assaulted.

One week after the L.A. arrest, police in New Orleans revealed that Sharper was under investigation for a rape reported by a woman who met the player at a bar following the Saints home win over Arizona on September 22, 2013.

WHAT FOLLOWED...

Sharper was formally charged by Los Angeles prosecutors on February 14. It was revealed that in addition to the allegations put forth by investigators in L.A. and New Orleans, Sharper was also under investigation for rapes in Las Vegas, Nevada; Miami, Florida; and Tempe, Arizona.

The player's New Orleans attorney, Nandi Campbell, maintains the innocence of her client. "No evidence suggests or implies that a sexual assault occurred," Campbell said. "The totality of the witnesses' statements and the physical evidence support the police department and district attorney's decision not to file criminal charges at this time."

While out on bail, Sharper was re-arrested in Los Angeles on February 27 after a warrant was issued in the New Orleans case. Two weeks later, an Arizona grand jury indicted the player on two counts of sexual assault and three counts of administering dangerous drugs relating to an alleged incident that occurred in November 2013. Sharper, whose bail had been previously set at $1 million, was ordered to be held without bail.

As of spring 2014 charges against Sharper have yet to be filed in the Las Vegas and Miami cases.

It was revealed that in addition to the allegations put forth by investigators in L.A. and New Orleans, Sharper was also under investigation for rapes in Las Vegas, Nevada; Miami, Florida; and Tempe, Arizona.

ACKNOWLEDGEMENTS

The author would like to thank managing editor Andrew Podnieks, and also the people at Indigo for their support, particularly Ed Wilkinson and Dominic Stones. Thanks also to Kathryn Zante for her tireless efforts in the design process.

Stan Nieradka worked as a creative consultant. His research was invaluable. Debbie Elicksen and Terry Mercury provided terrific insight for the book's introduction.

All statistics were compiled from Pro-Football-Reference.com and Sports-Reference.com, both wonderful resources.

A mile high salute goes out to some of the biggest Broncos fans in the GTA: Curtis Cheam, Ian Steele, Aaron Gogishvili, and Kevin Gibson. Let's never speak of Super Bowl XLVIII again.

Love to my biggest fans, my family: Mom, Dad, Justin, Megan, Butch and, of course, Mel and Jim, who throw the best Super Bowl parties. I'm not a Giants fan, but thanks to your team for beating the Patriots twice.

PHOTO CREDITS